YOU and the LAW

E. Richard Churchill

and

Linda R. Churchill

J. WESTON
WALCH
PUBLISHER
Portland, Maine

1   2   3   4   5   6   7   8   9   10

ISBN 0-8251-3771-3

Copyright © 1976, 1989, 1998
J. Weston Walch, Publisher
P. O. Box 658 • Portland, Maine 04104-0658

Printed in the United States of America

Contents

Part III: You, Your Family, the Law, and Current News *90*

To the Teacher

You and the Law was written by teachers, for teachers, and at the request of teachers. Educators attending regional social studies conventions asked the publisher for discovery materials that dealt with the way the law affects today's teenagers. Nothing was available to help junior and senior high students learn about the law as it applies to them. *You and the Law* was written in answer to this need.

You and the Law may be used successfully in a number of situations. It might well become a part of a general social studies class. Government classes can make excellent use of it for a portion of the program. *You and the Law* lends itself to the mini-course concept. Guidance counselors will find it highly useful for individual students or small groups.

You and the Law can also be used in class-size groups. Discussion questions are provided, as are a number of activities designed to help the student better understand the law and our legal process. The second part of the book includes discovery materials dealing with specific legal difficulties common to teenagers. These pages may be used in any order. When class-size groups deal with this material, it is expected that all questions will be answered. If *You and the Law* is used with individuals, however, some questions might go unanswered. The same holds true for the activities in Part I. Not all activities need be done nor all questions answered in order for students to profit from *You and the Law*.

By the same token, don't feel limited to the activities and questions posed by the authors.

Students will have questions of their own that need answers. Teachers may want to devise their own projects in some areas.

A preview quiz and final quiz have been added to this updated edition of *You and the Law*.

The preview quiz asks students to identify twenty legal terms used in the text. No student is expected to be able to identify correctly more than a few of these terms before having studied the text. This quiz is intended to alert students to the fact that they have much to learn. It is suggested that students keep their corrected copies to refer to now and again as they progress through the text.

The final quiz appears at the end of the text to provide an overview of what students have learned about the law. Fifteen short cases are provided in this quiz. Following each case is a question with five possible answers. Instruct students to read each case, consider what they know about the law, and then select *all* correct answers from among the five given.

You and the Law provides both teacher and student with a broad background from which to approach a study of the law as it affects today's youth. It will serve as a starting point for independent research and class discussion. Feel free to adapt the material in any manner that will make the law more meaningful to your students.

E. Richard Churchill
Linda R. Churchill

Teaching Suggestions

Throughout *You and the Law*, students are given the opportunity to explore ways in which various laws apply to them as individuals. Many times students are asked to respond from personal experience or to make a value judgment. Other times they are asked to give definite legal facts or opinions or to mention local and state laws.

Because laws differ from place to place and even from one year to the next, it is not practical to provide an answer section that states definite answers to legal questions. There are, however, some teaching strategies that may prove helpful in regard to this problem.

Local ordinances are often available in softbound form from the city clerk at nominal cost or may even be available without charge to school classes. The same is true of traffic codes. By all means obtain one or more copies of your community's local ordinances and make them available to your classes.

The annotated statutes of your state are quite another situation. In the authors' home state, these books run to about two dozen large volumes. In some states, this set of volumes is much larger. Public and university libraries usually own a set of the state's annotated statutes. Students should be made aware of the location of such sets and encouraged to refer to them as a part of their responsibilities while using *You and the Law*.

An alternate possibility is simply to use the library's copier and reproduce selected pages from these statutes. State statutes are not covered by copyright so there is no impropriety in copying selected pages for classroom use. At five or ten cents per page, the cost is not overwhelming. Laminating such copies or mounting them on a sturdy backing will add greatly to their life and use.

Although attorneys, like the rest of us, are busy people and have only their time to sell, it may be possible for your students to arrange to talk with local attorneys concerning various legal questions. Local law students and public defenders are often available to meet with committees or classes from time to time. Not to be forgotten are judges and clerks in local and district courts.

Points to keep in mind regarding these human resources include the following:

1. Students should have definite questions in mind.
2. Definite time schedules should be set and met.
3. Attorneys, clerks, and others should be made aware that the meetings are voluntary on their part and that their time is viewed as a contribution to the local school students. This is assumed to be the case any time a school class is involved, but clarification in advance is far better than a misunderstanding that results in having a group of students billed for legal consultation.

Classes may engage in a variety of projects that help to gather information concerning local and state laws and their application. Among these projects are:

1. Attending court sessions as individuals or small groups.
2. Meeting with or corresponding with the district attorney's office, with public defenders, with various "storefront" legal aid societies, and so on.
3. Reading and summarizing specific areas of the law as contained in the annotated statutes of the state.
4. Reading and excerpting articles from any of a number of family legal encyclopedias and other such books available at local libraries.
5. Making available copies of such books and legal texts or casebooks to students in the classroom as part of their reference collection.

Throughout your use of *You and the Law,* encourage class discussion. Also encourage students to discuss questions outside of class with family, friends, and others interested in the law. Many interesting ideas and facts will emerge from such discussions.

As your students study local and state laws and how they apply to individuals, be sure they understand that laws change, as do societies. Court decisions and legislation bring almost daily changes to the law. Informed citizens do their best to remain abreast of changes in those laws that affect them and their families.

To the Student

One of the major goals of public education is to give the student information that will help in his or her daily living both as a youth and as an adult. In today's complicated world an understanding of the function and place of the law is perhaps as important as any other subject of study.

You and the Law is not intended for lawyers. It is intended for students who must live daily with the laws of our nation. These laws affect our lives from dawn until dark. Often they work to our advantage. At times they seem to hinder us in what we wish to do and accomplish. Always the law is there.

The law is not something you can learn about and then forget. It is constantly changing in response to societal changes. New laws appear daily. Old laws are changed, taken out of the law books, and sometimes just forgotten. Yet the idea behind the law remains the same. The law is an attempt to provide us with a guide for living. Within this guide we have certain freedoms and an equal or even greater number of responsibilities. It is only when we understand both our freedoms and responsibilities that we can begin to understand the law and let it help us in our living.

You and the Law was not written by lawyers. It was written by teachers who are also spouses and parents, and who were also once a part of the youth culture. The authors have a considerable understanding of the basis of our law but don't pretend to be legal experts. *You and the Law* is not a legal guide. You can't take it to court with you and read it to the judge.

You and the Law is intended to give you some background concerning the law and how it relates to us today. It begins by giving you some basic ideas about the different kinds of laws we have and our rights under these laws. Some of the failings of the law are mentioned. The law is not perfect. No matter how hard people try, there are always things about the law that do not live up to our needs and wishes.

As you read this basic information, there will be some questions to discuss and some projects to do, both within and outside the classroom. These are all intended to help you understand the law by asking as well as answering questions.

The second portion of this book (Parts II and III) contains a series of articles that help you practice the application of law to daily living. Each article deals with some area of the law that is of interest and importance to youths. This part of the book asks for more than just discussion of ideas. In this section, space is provided so you may write your ideas and understandings. Sometimes the information you need for this written work comes from the first part of this book. At other times, some of the answers will come from the glossary at the end of the book. At times you will have to ask some questions and perhaps do some searching outside school to come up with answers that satisfy you. When you have completed this part of the book, you should know a lot more than you do now about some of the laws that affect you.

The third section of the book is just for reference. It is a glossary of legal terms. Only a few of the thousands of legal terms are defined here. If you need more definitions, your public library probably has some sort of legal dictionary. If the glossary uses a word you don't understand, look that word up in a regular dictionary. Each time you look up a word in the glossary, try to remember the word and its meaning. You will be pleased and surprised to discover how many of these words you meet in the daily newspaper and on television.

The material in the three sections of *You and the Law* is just enough to give you the beginning of an understanding of our laws. The authors haven't even attempted to explain the laws of your state or city. Laws vary so much from place to place that even attorneys often hire local attorneys to help them in trying cases away from home. However, the basic ideas behind the law are the same all over our nation. Once you have an understanding of these basic ideas, you are likely to be able to live within the law—unless you set out to do otherwise.

Nearly all libraries have materials on legal matters. Most county seats have a legal library in the county courthouse. These sources of information are available to you, even though it may be necessary for your teacher to make arrangements for you to use some of these materials.

Other sources of information are your local law enforcement officials. City police, county sheriffs, and state patrol officers can give you lots of information concerning various rights and responsibilities and general legal matters. If you ask for help and make appointments, most law enforcement agencies will go out of their way to help you understand the laws and how they are enforced. The better informed the citizens are, the easier it is to enforce and administer the laws of the city, state, or nation.

Another excellent source of information is the local legal profession. Lawyers are busy people. Their time is valuable. However, in every town there are lawyers who are willing to come to the classroom and speak on topics you suggest. If your teacher and class plan in advance, you probably can have several attorneys speak to your class while you are studying this book. A good understanding of the law helps lawyers help you.

A fourth source of information on the law is the daily newspaper. In fact, this source is likely to be the most interesting. There are daily police and court reports in many newspapers. Start reading these and bring them to class for a legal  bulletin board. Some of the things you read may surprise, puzzle, anger, or even frighten you. From these brief readings alone you may discover things about the law that are entirely new ideas for you.

There are also the newspaper features and stories. It is just about impossible to pick up a newspaper of any size that does not contain at least one article dealing with some area of the law. Some of these stories are amusing. Others are sad. Some will probably fill you with a feeling of injustice and cause you to wonder whether the law has failed. Collect these stories, bring them to class, and discuss them.

Preview Quiz

> **Directions:** As you read about the law and how it applies to you, you will encounter many legal terms. Some you already know and understand. Others will be new to you. At times you may discover there is more to the definition of a legal term than you now realize.
>
> In this short quiz twenty legal terms have been defined. Read each definition and then, in the space provided, write the legal term defined. Don't worry if you are certain about only a few answers. At this point you aren't supposed to be able to give correct terms for most of the definitions in this quiz.
>
> Answer as many questions as you can. Then check your answers. You may wish to keep this quiz handy as you learn about the law and how it applies to you. Look back at this quiz occasionally to see how many terms you can now identify. It is one way to tell how your understanding of the law is growing as you study.

1. _____ Anyone who knows about a crime or who conceals evidence of a crime.

2. _____ The illegal theft or stealing of another person's property.

3. _____ Publishing written or drawn material meant to harm someone's reputation.

4. _____ A legal order requiring an individual to appear in court.

5. _____ Anyone who testifies before a court.

6. _____ False writing or changing something written with intent to defraud.

7. _____ A group of citizens selected to hear evidence in court.

8. _____ An attempt or threat to physically harm a person.

9. _____ Breaking into someone's home with the intent to commit a crime.

10. _____ Saying false things about a person in public that may hurt his or her reputation.

11. _____ When someone accused of a crime is brought to court to hear the charges and to plead guilty or not guilty.

12. _____ A jury's decision.

13. _____ A less serious crime than a felony.

14. _____ Taking another's personal property or money by use of violence or threat of violence.

15. _____ A written law for a town or city.

16. _____ Failure to use reasonable care.

17. _____ A dishonest act intended to deprive another person of his or her rights or property.

18. _____ Stealing personal property that the owner has entrusted someone to care for.

19. _____ When two or more people agree to commit an illegal act.

20. _____ Deliberately burning or having a house or building burned.

What the Law Means

Introduction

Part I of *You and the Law* contains sections that give some of the reasons we have laws and how the law works. Each of these sections poses some questions to discuss or to research. These questions are intended to help you begin to think about the law.

The material given in this part of *You and the Law* provides you with some background information about the law. Most public libraries and many school libraries have books that tell much more about the law and how it works. When you want to know more than *You and the Law* explains, check out a book from the library and read the parts explaining the portion of the law that interests you.

Don't be upset if your class cannot agree on what is correct or incorrect in some of the discussion questions. That is why we have courts in our nation. Lawyers often do not agree on what the law says or how it should be applied. Even judges do not agree at times. This is one of the reasons why we have courts of appeal. When lawyers and judges don't agree, a higher court can help to decide the issue.

As you read and discuss, you and your classmates will probably decide that the law is not perfect. There may be times when you will decide the law is completely wrong. This may be true, at least from your point of view. Keep in mind, however, that the law tries hard to protect the rights of all of us. When such a difficult task is undertaken, some mistakes are bound to be made. When a mistake has been made, it is your duty and ours to try to change the law, not to break it. It is only when we try to improve the law that it can help preserve our rights and freedom.

1. The Law—Rules for Living in a Society

Our lives are filled with rules. Sometimes it seems we are about to be buried in rules. Yet without these rules, we would find living difficult, if not impossible. As our way of life becomes more complicated and society becomes more complex, we are faced with more and more laws to guide our lives.

People of old lived by what we might call "natural laws." They had to find enough food or they starved. They had to find a way to keep warm or they froze. If a conflict arose between two or more individuals, the stronger or perhaps the more clever person won. The loser most likely died. The individual either found a way to survive or died.

When people began to gather together into tribes or clans, and later into villages, their lives became more complicated. Living closely and in groups, they soon found that more rules were needed in order for people to get along with one another. These early rules or laws generally applied to one tribe or one city. They most often had to do with protection of property and grew out of the need for orderly living. One or more elders of the group remembered the group's rules and told others of them. These same elders decided how to punish anyone who broke the laws.

As the population grew and people became farmers, and then merchants and other specialists, the need for laws became greater. Laws were made to cover trade and commerce. Two distinct kinds of laws came into use. *Civil laws* applied to the way people got along in areas of business, property ownership, and daily living. *Criminal laws* covered acts of violence, theft, and other crimes against people. Under civil law, a person who did wrong had to make good that wrong. Under criminal law, the wrongdoer was punished.

Naturally, the increasing number of laws made it difficult for any one person to remember all these rules. In order to solve this problem, a Babylonian ruler, Hammurabi, about 1800 B.C. decided to codify the laws. The Code of Hammurabi became a written set of laws. They were cut into stone so that all who could read would know the law. Those who could not read could have the law read to them. Not only did this make it possible for all to know the law, but it also made certain that the law did not change because of someone's bad memory. Hammurabi's ideas concerning written laws and set punishments are the same ideas law writers use today.

The laws of Hammurabi were the kind we know as *edicts*. Edicts are made by the strongest person or the ruler. Once they are made, they become the law. Laws of this type date back to our earliest civilization and have continued for thousands of years. Even today, many laws come in the form of edicts. When Indian Prime Minister Indira Gandhi decided her political opponents were pushing her too hard in 1975, she made an edict. Her edict allowed the police and army to arrest and imprison anyone who did not agree with her. In today's society, most of us don't like edicts, but they still occur in government and in other areas of our daily living.

From the time of Hammurabi on, the idea of sets of written standard laws has been accepted. Each nation developed its own set of laws. When a stronger nation conquered a weaker one, the laws of the victor became the laws of the loser. When religion  became dominant, the Church often added its own set of laws to be followed.

Gradually people began to suspect that edicts were not always the best kind of laws.

Why should laws favor the ruler and the ruler's friends? Shouldn't the people have a voice in making laws?

In England in 1215, a document signed by King John gave some of the people a voice in making laws. This document was the Magna Carta. It was written to take some power away from the king and give certain powers to the nobility of England. Even though it did not give any rights to the poor, the Magna Carta was the beginning of laws granting human liberty. Among its ideas was that justice could not be bought and sold. The Magna Carta also demanded a fair and legal trial for people accused of crimes. Also included was the idea that taxes could not be collected by force, but only by legal means.

Soon, judges began making laws themselves in an interesting way. When a judge decided a case according to his understanding of the written laws, that judge's decision was often followed by other judges. We call such original decisions *precedents*. Much of our modern law is decided because of precedent. This sort of law became known as *common law* in England. English common law has had much to do with the laws by which we live today.

In the years following the signing of the Magna Carta, the rich and powerful people began to have more to say about the laws. Even the common people began to have a voice in lawmaking. The rights of the people became more important in laws that were passed.

By the time the United States declared its freedom and was ready to write a constitution, many people were concerned with the rights of the individual. This is why the Bill of Rights was added to the U.S. Constitution.

Today our legal system follows definite patterns. We have libraries of laws that were made to help us live together in a reasonable and just manner. Our civil laws and civil courts are set up to guide people in their relationships with one another. The civil law settles disputes between individuals and provides ways to right legal wrongs. Criminal laws and courts handle wrongdoings against society. Even though the crime may have harmed only one person, it is still considered a crime against all of society. For this reason, each person hires his or her own lawyer in a civil suit. In a criminal case, the person accused of a crime gets his or her lawyer, and the government hires the prosecutor to represent the people.

Even though they are based on logical ideas, our laws are often quite complicated. No book can explain the law entirely as it affects you. That is the job of a lawyer. This book can, however, help you to understand some of your obligations and responsibilities under the law. In thinking about the law, keep the following legal facts in mind.

The U.S. Constitution is the highest law of our land. Laws passed by the U.S. Congress can become part of the Constitution if they are passed as constitutional amendments. Next come state constitutions and laws. No state, though, can pass a law that goes against the U.S. Constitution, or laws of the United States. At the next level are county and local constitutions and laws. Again, these rules cannot go against either state or federal rules.

EXERCISES	• So that the facts we have just discussed become clearer, here are a few things committees of students might look up and report to the class.

1. What were some of the laws Hammurabi made? How did his punishments compare with those of today?

2. How did the Magna Carta happen to be signed? How well did it work?

3. Our Bill of Rights is made up of the first ten amendments to the Constitution of the United States. Read these amendments and rephrase them so that everyone in the class can understand them. Discuss the Bill of Rights as a group and decide how important it is to each of us today.

2. When Is a Crime Not Called a Crime?

When a person gets into difficulties with the police or other law enforcement groups, his or her problems come under the criminal laws of the state. When a person has difficulties over business deals, property, debts, and the like, those problems belong in the civil courts. As a rule, *criminal acts* may end up with a person going to jail. *Civil acts* may result in changed actions or payment of damages.

Let's talk about criminal difficulties. Most important crimes are called *felonies*. A felony is a crime that is considered serious and may result in a prison sentence. Crimes not considered quite so serious are called *misdemeanors*. These may be punished by a jail sentence, a fine, or both. Felony convictions usually call for prison sentences of over a year. Convictions for misdemeanors are likely to result in a jail sentence of less than a year.

A strange thing about the law is that some things called misdemeanors may actually seem more serious and dangerous than others called felonies. Both are crimes and require the accused person to defend himself against the government. Felonies require major trials, while misdemeanors may demand fairly simple trials.

If a person buys property that she knows is stolen, she is guilty of a felony. A person accused of receiving stolen property will receive a major court trial and may go to prison for several years if found guilty. Her neighbor may be arrested by the highway patrol for driving 120 miles an hour through a school zone after having had three drinks too many. Normally this offense is called a misdemeanor. The accused can get by with a simple trial before a traffic judge in many states. If she is found guilty, she will pay a fine, probably get a warning from the judge, and perhaps lose her driver's license for a short time.

Many people believe the drunk driver is far more dangerous to society than is the person who receives stolen goods. Under our criminal law, this is not considered to be the case. For this reason, many people find our laws to be imperfect. The law tries to protect us all equally. It sometimes fails.

Usually, the difference between a felony and a misdemeanor makes pretty good sense. Crimes of violence and deliberate crimes against people and property are generally felonies.

EXERCISES	• As a class, decide which of the following are most likely felonies and which are probably misdemeanors.

1. Theresa wanted nice things. Most of all she wanted nice clothing and jewelry. One day she decided that the time had come for her to have the things she had always wanted. Later that evening, she threw a brick through the window of a jewelry store. From inside the broken window she pulled a beautiful necklace and four diamond rings.

2. When things went poorly for Dan, he tended to lose his head. This had been one of those times. The whole day had gone badly. Now he decided it was someone else's turn to have a bad day. Without thinking, Dan threw his half-filled soda can into the windshield of a car parked at the curb. When the can hit, a web of cracks appeared on the expensive windshield.

3. Susan knew the town of Riverdale had started a crackdown on dogs. Just the night before, she read an article about dog control. Anyone whose dog was caught would have to pay a fine and perhaps go to jail. When the doorbell rang, Susan saw a police officer on the porch. In his right hand he held a rope. At the other end of the rope was Susan's dog, Spot.

4. Roger hadn't meant to do anything wrong. It was just that he needed more money than he had in order to pay his bills and do the things that needed doing. Every few days, he was able to take a few dollars out of the company cash register. This went on for more than two years before the boss caught on.

5. The city of Highview had very strict laws. One of the laws had to do with overtime parking. Francine never seemed able to park without coming back to find a ticket stuck under her car's wiper blade. It didn't seem fair for this to keep happening to her. After she had paid half a dozen parking tickets, Francine decided to stop worrying about them. After six unpaid tickets had accumulated in her glove compartment, she received a registered letter. The letter informed her that if she did not appear in traffic court on the following Thursday afternoon, a police officer would be sent to arrest her.

6. Louise was subpoenaed to appear as a witness in a trial. Her friend, Howard, was on trial for selling illegal drugs. Louise had no intention of saying anything that would hurt Howard. When she was asked questions about Howard, Louise gave false answers if she thought the truth might harm Howard. A subsequent witness proved Louise had lied.

7. Bill liked to think he was the sort of fellow nobody ever pushed around. One evening, he took his girl to an amusement park. While there, Bill got into an argument with three men. As Bill and his girl were leaving the park, Bill spotted the same guys in the parking lot. Bill went to his car, unlocked the trunk, and took out his jack handle. A minute later, one of the men had a six-inch gash in his head, and the other two were backing away.

3. Not All People in Court Are Criminals

Because we have two basic kinds of law, we have two different types of court cases. As you now know, in a *criminal* case the suspect must defend himself against charges brought by the government. Usually that government is the state government, but it can also be local or federal. In a *civil case*, one individual is bringing charges against another individual. Both sides involved furnish their own attorneys. The government is not directly involved in the case.

Civil courts came into being as hearing places for civil law violations. As society got to the stage of trading and specialization, disagreements between people arose. An entire branch of law developed to help solve such difficulties. As society grew and became more complicated, civil law had to become more complex as it tried to keep up with all the problems.

Civil cases eventually began to include disputes between people and companies, and between one company and another. Under some circumstances, even branches of the government got involved in civil court cases, either as the side bringing the suit or the side being sued.

The object of a civil court case is to right a wrong. This may come about through payment of money called *damages*. It may come when a person or persons stop doing something they have been doing. At times it involves returning things to the way they once were. Such problems are called *torts* and involve all cases dealing with injuries to a person, to things owned by a person, or to a person's reputation. It is in civil courts that you sue or are sued.

What begins as a civil case may be found also to involve a criminal act. When this happens, the criminal courts may become involved as a result of what has happened in the civil court.

Unless you set out deliberately to break the law, you are not likely to become involved in criminal courts (except for traffic courts). In today's complicated world you may very well end up in civil court. You may go to a civil court because you *want* to, not because you *have* to. Many things that affect us can end up in civil court. Millions of people every year find themselves in court; this does not make them criminals, even if they lose their cases. It just means that they became involved in a dispute that needed the court to act as umpire or referee.

Let's follow an individual through the court procedure. Joe paid to have some construction work done, but it was not done correctly. A number of letters, phone calls, and personal visits to the contractor followed. No matter what Joe said or did, he could not convince the contractor to correct his sloppy work.

Finally Joe went to his lawyer. The lawyer told Joe that he could not sue the contractor to correct his work. However, Joe could bring suit to recover or get back the cost of fixing up the messy job. Joe decided to sue. He told his lawyer exactly what was wrong and what he had done in his efforts to get the contractor to cooperate.

The lawyer asked Joe for copies of the letters he had sent to the contractor, the canceled check with which Joe had paid for the work, and the original contract Joe had signed with the contractor. He also asked Joe to list as accurately as he could the dates he had called the contractor or had visited with him. Joe also wrote out a complete description of what was wrong with the job. Once this material was assembled, the lawyer studied it and decided that Joe could probably win his suit.

The next day, Joe's lawyer went to the county civil court and filed a *complaint* with the court clerk. In this complaint the lawyer gave the facts in the case, named the contractor as *defendant*, and stated that suit was being brought for $7,000 to pay for repairing the mess plus the court costs and attorney's fees. Once the complaint was signed, it was given a number called a *docket number*. From then on, this docket number would always be referred to when anything happened concerning Joe's suit against the contractor.

Joe's attorney also requested a jury trial. He told Joe that jury trials weren't always desirable and that they did cost special fees and took more time. In this case he thought it worth the extra effort because so many people were tired of being cheated. The attorney believed that some jury members would be sympathetic toward Joe and side with him.

After the complaint had been filed, the court clerk prepared a copy of the complaint, a *summons*, and an *answer form*. These were given to the county sheriff, who sent a deputy to serve the papers on the contractor. Once the papers were served, the deputy filled out a form, which he returned to the court clerk. The form stated that the papers had been given personally to the defendant.

The summons told the contractor how long he had to prepare his answer to the complaint. In the answer he and his lawyer would try to prove to the court that the suit was not justified. This answer had to be returned to the court by the date mentioned in the summons. If the contractor did not file his answer or appear before the court, Joe would win his suit by default, in other words, he wouldn't have to go through with the trial.

On the date shown on the summons, both Joe and the contractor went to court with their attorneys. The contractor's attorney presented her client's answer and pleaded "not guilty" for the contractor. The judge had the court clerk enter the plea and set a date for the trial.

To prepare for the case, both lawyers made sure they had all the documents that applied to the matter. Both lawyers inspected the job done by the contractor and took pictures of it. Joe's lawyer hired another contractor to inspect the job and make an estimate on the cost of repair.

The second contractor agreed the work had been poorly done and said he would be a witness for the *plaintiff* (Joe).

Joe's attorney said that they were lucky. Quite often, a merchant or tradesperson will not testify against another in the same business. This was one reason it was hard to win cases against contractors and mechanics.

When Joe talked to a lumberyard employee, the man told him that Joe's contractor had requested cheaper materials for Joe's job. This saved the contractor money even though he charged Joe for first-class materials. Joe asked the lumberyard employee to be his witness, but the man refused because he could not get time off from work to testify. Joe told his attorney. The attorney got the court to issue a *subpoena* to the worker. This forced his employer to give him time off to come to court. Of course, Joe had to pay a witness fee, but he felt it was worth it to have the man as his witness.

The day before the trial, the contractor's attorney called Joe's lawyer and offered to settle for $1,000. Joe's lawyer asked Joe if he wanted to settle for that amount. Joe decided he would rather go to trial. His attorney agreed, and the offer of settlement was refused.

When the day of the trial arrived, Joe was nervous. He had never been to court before, and it was all new and strange to him. After the judge had made sure both Joe and the contractor were in court, the jury was chosen. Joe was surprised to find that about thirty possible or prospective jurors had been called to court that day. He also was surprised to learn that his trial would have only six jurors. His lawyer explained that not all cases had twelve jurors. About half of the prospective jurors were called by the court. They identified themselves and answered some questions the judge asked. Then the two attorneys began choosing the trial jury. Each lawyer could ask a prospective juror questions. From time to time, the lawyers got rid of jurors by "challenging" them. The contractor's attorney challenged two people who said they had experienced bad dealings with contractors. Joe's lawyer had one juror dismissed because he was a friend of the contractor. Within a few

more minutes, the jury was chosen. All those possible jurors not chosen were then sent home.

From then on, the trial was pretty much like Joe had seen on TV, except that the lawyers didn't do any shouting or acting. Joe's case was explained. The documents Joe had given his attorney were presented as evidence and numbered by the court clerk. Each document was explained, including the friendly contractor's estimate of the cost of repair.

Joe's witnesses were called and were asked questions by Joe's attorney. Once the judge asked a question of his own. After each witness testified, the contractor's attorney asked questions in cross-examination. She tried to get the witnesses to say things that would help the contractor's case.

Joe himself took the stand and told his side of the story. He too was cross-examined by the contractor's attorney. Several times the attorney asked Joe whether he was an expert at home repairs. Joe admitted he wasn't, which seemed to please the contractor's lawyer.

Then the contractor's lawyer gave his side of the case. His witnesses included two character witnesses who told how long they had known the contractor and that they felt he was an honest man. Joe's attorney asked each of them only a couple of questions in cross-examination. Of each, he asked, "Have you ever done construction work?" and "Has the contractor ever built for you?" When they said "no" to both questions, Joe's lawyer seemed pleased.

At the end of the trial, both lawyers spent a few minutes summing up their side of the case. Each tried to convince the jury that he or she was right. Then the judge instructed the jury on the law and  explained that they could decide that Joe was either right or wrong. If they decided Joe was right, they could award the full amount of damages Joe had asked for, or a smaller amount.

The jury deliberated only a short time before they reached a decision. They decided in favor of Joe for the full amount of his request.

Joe was happy, but his attorney told him it wasn't over yet. The contractor might refuse to pay, or he might be unable to pay. In that case, Joe would have to get the court to issue a *writ of execution*. That document would let the sheriff seize money or property to pay the judgment. This would take time and effort. It might just happen that all of the contractor's property was exempt from seizure because it might legally belong to his wife, or it might be personal property, which the law says cannot be taken away to pay judgments.

The attorney also told Joe that the contractor might appeal to a higher court, in which case the whole trial would have to be repeated. It would be ten days before they knew whether an appeal had been filed.

Now that you have some idea of how a civil court suit might operate, it is a good time for your teacher to arrange for some students to visit a civil court trial. After the visit, the students can tell the rest of the class what they saw and heard and how closely the trial followed Joe's case against the contractor.

EXERCISES

- Following are some situations that led to court appearances. Read them and decide as a class whether the court involved was criminal or civil.

1. When Ted and Alice were married, they were so much in love that neither could believe their feelings would ever change. During the next five years, though, their feelings did change. Now it seemed they fought constantly. Finally Alice filed for divorce. The next thing Ted knew, he was in court with his lawyer, trying to keep from losing the house, the car, the bank account, and their two sons to Alice.

2. Jim saved for over a year to buy a car. Then he spent a month visiting used-car lots, trying out different models. Finally he decided on a four-year-old economy model. The day Jim drove his first car home, he was elated. That was the only happy day Jim had with the car. It took every cent Jim could earn just to repair the car as things broke down. Finally a mechanic told Jim what was wrong. The car had been badly wrecked before Jim bought it. In addition, its engine was from a different auto put out by another company.

3. When Joyce became involved in politics, she began to spend all of her free time helping members of her party with their campaigns. As it happened, Joyce's boss was also involved in politics. The party he supported was not Joyce's party though. Several times he mentioned to Joyce that she was working for the wrong party. Joyce just laughed and said, "We'll let the voters decide which is the right party." On election day, Joyce's party won a victory. The following day, Joyce's boss fired her.

4. Larry was always willing to take a dare. When some of his friends suggested he ride through the city flower gardens on his bicycle at midnight, he was quick to accept. Word spread, and on the night Larry was to perform, several dozen friends showed up to watch. Larry had made several passes through the flower gardens when suddenly a red light atop a police cruiser began a steady blink, blink, blink. Larry ran for it, but after ten minutes and six miles, three police cruisers cornered him in a dead-end alley.

5. When Mildred and Tom sold their house, they got a down payment of $5,000 and "carried" the rest of the amount due. Each month the new owners were to pay Tom and Mildred $700 for interest and principal. After a year and a half, the payments stopped. When Tom became worried and checked on the new owners, he found they had already moved out of the house. When Tom went inside, what he saw made him feel sick. Every wall was damaged, the kitchen was a wreck, the carpets were ruined, and the whole house needed repainting. Tom figured the total repair cost to be well over $9,000.

6. Sue's dog was a good pup in every way except one. He refused to stay at home. Sue had a fence built, but the hound dug out. She put him on a chain, but he almost hanged himself on the porch railing. Finally Sue

gave up and let him go where he wanted. One day he got into a fight with the neighbor's champion show dog on the neighbor's lawn. When the two dogs were separated, Sue's dog was clearly the winner. He didn't have a scratch on him, but the other dog lost an ear in the fight.

7. A tremendous crash jolted Albert and Sara awake with a start. A driver had lost control of his car on the curve in front of their house, and now his car was in their living room. Several days later Albert learned that the driver had no insurance. Worse, Albert's insurance company told him that the terms of his insurance policy did not obligate the company to cover the loss.

8. George noticed that the check he had just received from Ted was not filled in completely. The amount of $100 was there in numbers, but not in words. George studied the check and decided he could very easily add another zero to the amount. Then he wrote in $1,000 in words. To his delight the bank cashed the check.

4. When Do You Need a Lawyer?

How many times have you heard someone say, "I'm going to sue you"? For every time you have heard those threats, how many times have they been carried out? How many people who threaten to sue realize that the act of suing does *not* necessarily mean collecting? It's up to a judge and perhaps a jury to decide whether a sued person has to pay any damages.

The threat of being sued, arrested, taken to court, or sent to jail is always present in modern society. Fortunately, many people go through life without ever having to appear in court. Quite a few even manage to avoid hiring a lawyer. Other people spend vast amounts of time and money consulting lawyers. Most of these individuals have never deliberately broken a law and aren't even involved in court cases. They simply depend upon lawyers for advice and help as a part of their everyday business.

For most of us, it is hard to decide when we need a lawyer's advice. It has been said that all a lawyer has for sale is her time. This is true in that lawyers make their living by spending time helping others solve their legal difficulties or avoid having legal problems. Therefore, lawyers have to charge for their services. If they represent you in court, you expect to pay for their services. When attorneys file legal papers for you or examine documents, you are charged a fee. Even when you talk to a lawyer on the telephone, you probably will get a bill.

Lawyers' bills often are a surprise to people who infrequently need legal services. Many people give quite serious thought to attorneys' fees and therefore don't make appointments to see lawyers. Others don't call attorneys because they don't realize when they need them. Of all questions concerning a person's relationship with the law, this may well be the most important. When does a person need the help of an attorney? It is almost as important to know when a lawyer is not needed as when one *is*.

EXERCISES	• Read the scenarios that follow. Discuss the reasons why a lawyer might or might not be necessary in each situation. Keep in mind the expense of consulting a lawyer. Also consider the possible problems that might arise if you yourself tried to handle something that really needed a lawyer.

1. The doorbell rings one evening, and when you answer the door, a man hands you a legal-looking piece of paper called a summons. It tells you to appear before the court to answer charges brought against you by a man with whom you have done business.
2. You have decided to buy a new car. In order to finance it, you have to sign an agreement to make monthly payments to repay the loan, interest on the loan, and insurance. The payments are to continue for thirty-six months.
3. An insurance salesperson has talked you into buying an insurance policy that will pay your family $50,000 if you die or get killed. You will have to make payments until you are sixty-five (if you live that long).
4. Your father and mother hav e decided to write a will so that there will be no question about which children get what in the event either parent dies.
5. Another driver ran a stop sign and you hit him. Fortunately, you were not injured. The other driver wasn't so lucky. He suffered a broken back and internal injuries. His doctor says the man probably will never be able to walk again. The injured man says you could have avoided the accident if you had tried.
6. You and your spouse have found exactly the house you want. It is within your price range, in the part of town you like best, and in great condition. You are ready to make an offer through the real estate agent.
7. Jane and Lois have decided to open a gift shop and have invited you to join them as a partner. A good location is available. A number of supply houses are ready to fill the shelves with gifts for the three of you to sell.
8. It is income tax time again. No matter how many times you read the tax form instructions, they just don't make sense. A friend mentions that you can go to prison if you don't fill out your tax returns properly.

5. But I Can't Afford a Lawyer

Needing a lawyer and being able to afford one may be two entirely different things. Supreme Court rulings have established that everyone who is accused of a crime is entitled to a lawyer. In addition, an accused person may have a lawyer present even during police questioning. The courts have ruled that people who can't afford lawyers should have the same protection as people who can.

In order to protect the rights of the poor in court, *public defenders* are used. Public defenders are lawyers who are paid from public funds to defend poor people accused of crimes. This system of providing attorneys for poor people who have criminal charges filed against them

has done much to ensure everyone's rights to protection under the law.

In spite of the good that public defenders can do, the system has a serious fault: In general, public defenders deal only with defense against criminal charges. Some large cities now have *legal aid societies*, which are organized to provide legal advice for people who can't pay for legal services. Lawyers working for legal aid societies not only defend against criminal suits but also help out in defense of civil suits.

A source of legal aid for the poor, which has appeared in recent years, is the *neighborhood legal aid group*. Attorneys in these groups help the poor not only with criminal matters but with civil cases as well—such as, disputes with landlords, loan companies, merchants, schools, and so on. Lawyers who are a part of these groups often provide legal services for little or no fee.

Closely associated with the neighborhood legal aid office is the *Rural Legal Services Office.* This organization was formed as the result of government concern for people in basically rural areas who might be unable to obtain legal help. Rural legal aid groups are free to those who cannot afford to pay for legal help.

The interesting thing about neighborhood and rural legal aid groups is that they help in both civil and criminal matters. In addition to defending their clients from suits, they also bring suits for their clients. This opens up an entirely new area of legal help for the nation's poor. The ability to bring suit as well as to be defended from suit or prosecution adds a tremendous amount of protection to the poor.

Many citizens cannot afford the services of a lawyer for fairly small civil cases but earn too much to qualify for legal aid society help. For these people there are two possible sources of legal aid. Some areas offer a *Lawyer Referral Service.* This group is set up by the lawyers in the area. Its purpose is to help provide a lawyer who

is willing to take cases for whatever the client can afford to pay. A second source of help is the *county civil court* or *small claims court.* In these courts, a person can bring suit or can defend himself without the help of a lawyer. These courts are for the person who is involved in a civil suit where the amount of money is fairly small. In the authors' home state, these courts deal with cases involving claims up to a few thousand dollars. Such courts have clerks who explain the forms that must be filed and help either party get the case going. Neither the judge nor the clerks of the court act as attorneys, however. Sometimes the judges will give advice on proper legal conduct. In such courts, the parties to the suit handle the entire procedure on their own, from filing their complaints to conducting their trials. Some courts either provide a guide to handling one's own case or can tell where to obtain such a guide.

Even with these sources of legal help, many citizens still do not receive the legal aid to which they may be entitled. This may be because they are not aware of the available help or because such help is not available where they live. In spite of such shortcomings, we are closer today to providing legal protection for all citizens than we were a few years ago.

| **EXERCISES** | • As a class, divide into committees to discover what legal services are available to the poor and near poor where you live. Compile a list of these services and a description of the legal aid each offers. Discuss the findings in class. Be sure to get copies of any printed materials that describe the groups' services or explain how to act as your own attorney. |

Review Quiz I

A. True or False

Directions: Read each question carefully, and then write either "T" (true) or "F" (false) in the space provided.

1. _____ Edicts are rules or laws made by a ruler or the most powerful person in a group or society.

2. _____ The Magna Carta gave new powers to the king of England in 1215.

3. _____ Although a criminal act may harm only one person, it is considered to be a crime against society.

4. _____ In a civil court case each side obtains its own attorney.

5. _____ All civil court cases result in the payment of damages.

6. _____ A complaint is filed before a suit comes to trial in civil court.

7. _____ The individual or company who files a civil suit is known as the plaintiff.

8. _____ Civil court cases always use juries composed of twelve jurors.

9. _____ Only the attorney for the defendant is allowed to cross-examine witnesses in a civil trial.

10. _____ A writ of execution allows a sheriff to execute a guilty person.

11. _____ A person who is sued must pay damages to the one bringing the suit.

12. _____ It is a good idea to consult an attorney before signing any document or sales agreement.

13. _____ Public defenders deal with defending the poor in criminal cases but do not represent them in civil cases.

14. _____ Legal aid societies are allowed only to defend against suits but cannot file suits for their clients.

15. _____ Only the defendant is allowed to have an attorney in small claims court.

B. Sentence Completions

Directions: Underline the one answer in parentheses which makes that statement correct.

16. Acts of violence and crimes against people are covered by (*civil, criminal*) law.

17. Judges' decisions are called (*edicts, precedents*) and are often followed by other judges.

18. More important or major crimes are called (*misdemeanors, felonies*).

19. Problems that result in civil court trials are called (*damages, torts*).

20. A civil court summons allows a defendant a certain amount of time in which to file his or her (*complaint, answer*).

21. A (*summons, subpoena*) forces a witness to come to court.

22. A request to have a higher court reconsider the decision of a lower court is (*an appeal, a writ of execution, a verdict*).

23. In a small claims court trial the (*judge, lawyer*) may give advice on legal conduct.

24. English (*civil, common, criminal*) law has affected many of today's laws.

25. Every case that comes before a civil court is given a (*complaint, summons, docket*) number.

6. Ignorance of the Law Is No Excuse

About four thousand years ago, some trader was probably brought before a village elder and accused of cheating a woman by selling her less grain than she paid for. The frightened trader begged forgiveness, saying, "I am from another town. I did not understand your laws." The stern elder looked at the trader and replied, "Your ignorance of the law is no excuse. It is your responsibility to understand our laws." Five minutes later, the unlucky trader was taken to the village square and his right hand was cut off.

It was exactly this sort of thing Hammurabi hoped to avoid when he had the laws written. With written laws, everyone had a chance to learn the laws. Once you knew the law and understood it, you could either live by the law or suffer the consequences. That is the position courts and judges have held since laws were made and enforced.

Ignorance of the law is no excuse for not obeying the law. This is true in your local police court, in county or state courts, and in federal courts. It is your duty as a citizen to know, understand, and obey the law. This is why laws have to be written after a lawmaking group makes them. In that way, every citizen is able to know and understand the law.

It is easy to see why lawbreakers are not allowed to plead ignorance of the law. If every criminal were allowed to say, "I did not know it was wrong," and go free, it wouldn't be long before our legal system lost all meaning. However, people do get into trouble at times because they don't know the law, or they don't understand it.

If all the laws of all the states, counties, and cities in the United States were put together, the books containing these laws would fill a freight train. Then, if all the laws of the federal government were added, the train probably would be too long to handle.

Aside from the great number of laws is the fact that legal wording isn't always easy to understand. Of course, common sense should tell a person some things are wrong. But no amount of common sense will help a person read some laws unless he or she is a highly trained lawyer. Below is an actual sample of a clearly written statute from the authors' home state. It is part of the state's law covering first-degree murder. Read it carefully. Be sure you understand what it says. The names and numbers tell where to locate previous court decisions that have a bearing on the law you are reading. Some of these decision may help make this law clearer. Some had to do with making the present law what it is. (These are known as precedents, if you remember.)

II. ELEMENTS OF FIRST DEGREE MURDER.

A. IN GENERAL.

Degrees of murder distinguished. The distinguishing feature between murder in the first degree and murder in the second degree is that to constitute murder in the first degree the jury must find "premeditation," whereas if said fact be not found, it is murder in the second degree. Kent v. People, 8 Colo. 563, 9 P. 852 (1885). See Carlson v. People, 91 Colo. 418, 15 P.2d 625 (1932).

Proof of killing alone is not murder. Proof of the mere abstract fact that the accused killed the deceased will not sustain a verdict of guilty of first or second degree murder based on instructions thereto. Leonard v. People, 149 Colo. 360, P.2d 54 (1962).

First degree murder is the deliberate and premeditated killing of a human being. Washington v. People, 158 Colo. 115, 405 P.2d 735 (1965), cert. denied, 383 U.S. 953, 86 S. Ct. 1217, 16 L Ed. 2d 215 (1966).

Murder in the first degree, other than in the commission of a felony, is the deliberate and premeditated killing of a human being. Hinton v. People, 169 Colo. 545, 458 P.2d 611 (1969), cert. denied, 397 U.S. 1047, 90 S. Ct. 1375, 25 L. Ed. 2d 659 (1970).

To constitute murder under a statute it is necessary that the killing be done in the mode described by the statute. Kent v. People, 8 Colo. 563, 9 P. 852 (1885).

It is not necessary to prove a motive as an essential element in the crime of murder. Armijo v. People, 134 Colo. 344, 304 P.2d 633 (1956).

Proof of a motive is not an essential part of the state's case in a murder prosecution. People v. Spinuzzi, 149 Colo. 391, 369 P.2d 427 (1962).

Death in course of unjustified arrest by private person. A private person who, without any excuse or justification, in order to accomplish the arrest of another not shown to have been guilty of any crime, shoots, merely intending to wound, is guilty of murder if the shot takes fatal effect. Demato v. People, 49 Colo. 147, 111 P. 703, 35 L.R.A. (n.s.) 621, 1912A Ann. Cas. 783 (1910).

B. PREMEDITATION.

Law review. For note, "The Role of Mental Disorder in Showing the Absence of Premeditation and Deliberation in Murder Trials," see 29 Rocky Mt. L. Rev. 396 (1957).

Premeditation required. To be guilty of murder of the first degree a person must not only be sane, but in killing he must have acted with premeditation. Ingles v. People, 92 Colo. 518, 22 P.2d 1109 (1933).

In order to make out first degree murder under this section, other than in commission of a felony, there is the requirement of a premeditated killing. Watkins v. People, 158 Colo. 485, P.2d 425 (1965).

Premeditation directed against one other than victim suffices. If shot is fired, without justification, and a killing results, the homicide is first degree murder, although the premeditation was directed against one other than the person actually killed. Ryan v. People, 50 Colo. 99, 114 P. 306, 1912B Ann. Cas. 1232 (1911).

Words such as "deliberate" and "premeditated" refer to the intention of the accused at the time of the killing. Hill v. People, 1 Colo. 436 (1872).

They are matters of inference and presumption. Premeditation and deliberation are matters of inference and presumption to be drawn by the jury from the facts and circumstances leading up to, surrounding, and explanatory of the homicide. Van

Houton v. People, 22 Colo. 53, 43 P. 137 (1895); Robinson v. People, 76 Colom 416, 232 P. 672 (1925).

Thus, intent may be inferred from act. Premeditation does not require positive proof of an intent prior to the commission of the act, as such prior intent may be inferred from the act. Robinson v. People, 76 Colo. 416, P. 672 (1925).

And malice, premeditation, and deliberation may be inferred from use of a deadly weapon. Hampton v. People, 171 Colo. 153, 465 P.2d 394 (1970); Lopez v. People, 175 Colo. 573, 488 P.2d 892 (1971).

Intent to kill and premeditation may be inferred from the intentional use of a deadly weapon in a deadly manner. Mills v. People, 146 Colo. 457, 362 P.2d 152 (1961), cert. denied, 369 U.S. 841, 82 S. Ct. 869, 7 L. Ed. 2d 846 (1962).

Where evidence established that defendant approached the deceased brandishing a gun after having threatened deceased's friends, and that a shot was fired, killing deceased, the jury could have found premeditation or lack of considerable provocation for killing. People v. Spinuzzi, 149 Colo. 391, 369 P.2d 427 (1962).

But not from mere blow by hand or fist. A conviction for first degree murder will not stand when the blow was struck on being aroused from sleep, probably in anger, but certainly without plan, deliberation, or premeditation. A blow with a fist and a fortiori with the open hand is not calculated to cause death to a person in good health and of mature age; death is not the natural consequence of such a blow. Stafford v. People, 154 Colo. 113, 388 P.2d 774 (1964).

Flight is not evidence of premeditation and deliberation. Stafford v. People, 154 Colo. 113, 388 P.2d 774 (1964).

Shortness of time between purpose and act immaterial. If one actually forms the purpose to kill another, premeditates upon it before performing the act, and then performs it, he is guilty of murder in the first degree no matter how short the time may have been between the purpose and its execution. Wickham v. People, 41 Colo. 345, 93 P. 478 (1907).

Time is not essential if there was a design and determination to kill formed in the mind of the defendant previous to or at the time the mortal wound was given. Van Houton v. People, 22 Colo. 53, 43 P. 137 (1885).

Premeditation requires time for one thought to follow another. No particular time need pass in order to establish deliberation and premeditation. The important thing is that there must be at least enough time to permit one thought to follow another. An impulsive killing cannot be first degree murder. The law does not demand that a defendant shall have premeditated for any period of time, but that the defendant shall have committed the act deliberately and with premeditation. Hammil v. People, 145 Colo. 577, 361 P.2d 117, cert. denied, 368 U.S. 903, 82 S. Ct. 182, 7 L. Ed. 2d 98 (1961); Bradney v. People, 162 Colo. 403, 426 P. 2d 765 (1967).

The deliberation and formed design need not have existed at the inception of the transaction which finally resulted in the homicide. It matters not how short the interval between the formation of the design and the death if it included the time necessary for one thought to follow another. People v. Spinuzzi, 149 Colo. 391, 369 P.2d 427 (1962).

The elements of deliberation and premeditation are established by proof of the formed design to kill, and length of time is not a determinative factor. The only time requirement for deliberation and premeditation within the meaning of the first degree murder statute is an interval sufficient for one thought to follow another. Hinton v. People, 169 Colo. 545, 458 P.2d 611 (1969), cert. denied, 397 U.S. 1047, 90 S. Ct. 1375, 25 L. Ed. 2d 659 (1970).

As to requirement of malice under former statute. See May v. People, 8 Colo. 210, 6 P. 816 (1885); Murphy v. People, 9 Colo., 435, 14 P. 528 (12886); Andrews v. People, 33 Colo. 193, 79 P. 1031, 108 Am St. R. 76 (1905); McAndrews v. People, 71 Colo. 542, 208 P. 486, 24 A.L.R. 655 (1922); Ingles v. People, 92 Colo. 518, 22 P.2d 1109 (1933); Baker v. People, 114 Colo. 50, 160 P.2d 983 (1945); Shreeves v. People, 126 Colo. 413, 249 P.2d 1020 (1952); Kukuljan v. People, 129 Colo. 116, 267 P.2d 1017 (1954); Beckstead v. People, 133 Colo. 72, 292 P.2d 189 (1956); Lutz v. People, 133 Colo. 229, 293 P.2d 646 (1956); Castro v. People, 140 Colo. 493, P.2d 1020 (1959); Smith v. People, 142 Colo. 523, 351 P.2d 457 (1950); People v. Spinuzzi, 149 Colo. 391, 369 P.2d 427 (1962); Stafford v. People, 154 Colo. 113, 388 P.2d 774 (1964); Balltrip v. People, 157 Colo. 108, 401 P.2d 259 (1965); Ferrin v. People, 164 Colo. 130, 433 P.2d 108 (1967); Gonzales v. People, 168 Colo. 545, 452 P.2d 46 (1969); Hinton v. People, 169 Colo. 545, 458 P.2d 611 (1969); cert. denied, 397 U.S. 1047, 90 S. Ct. 1375, 25 L. Ed. 2d 659 (1970); Hampton v. People, 171 Colo. 153, 465 P.2d 394 (1970); Moya v. People, 174 Colo. 435, 484 P.2d 788 (1971); Lopez v. People, 175 Colo. 503, 488 P.2d 892 (1971); Walker v. People, 175 Colo. 173, 489 P.2d 584 (1971); People v. Morant, — Colo.—499 P.2d 1173 (1972).

EXERCISES • Once you have read and understood the statute, rewrite it in your own words. Make certain your rewriting does not change the meaning of the law. Explain the law completely as you rewrite it.

In addition to the number of laws and their sometimes complicated wording, there is still another problem. Many laws were made years ago. As the world changed, the laws often did not. Thousands of out-of-date laws are still in the law books. Lawmakers try to keep up-to-date, but some of these old laws slip by until someone puts one of them to use. For example, until a few years ago, the citizens of a certain town were not allowed to buy liquor in their town. Neither were they allowed to keep liquor in their homes. An old town law said that any property owner who was found to have liquor in the home would have to give the house and land to the city.

Then there is still another difficulty in understanding the law. At times it is quite difficult to even get hold of the laws to read. One of the authors asked a city police clerk for a copy of the city traffic laws. The clerk told the author that the booklets containing the city traffic code were "for official use only" and not to be distributed to the public! A friend who asked the same question at a later date was able to obtain copies of the city traffic laws, but the booklet cost several dollars.

It is important to realize that we are surrounded by laws about which we may know nothing. Almost daily, new laws are made that affect us. Even lawyers have to check the written laws before they can advise clients.

- The following questions are provided to help you understand just how many laws affect you. Make this a class project in which each student or small group takes one question and answers it correctly and completely. Don't guess. Find the answer to share with the rest of the class. When you present your answer to the class, explain where you located the answer and how much time it took you to find it. Some of these questions will be simple; a few may give you trouble.

1. If you wanted to learn about the laws of your state, where could you get a complete set of up-to-date state laws, and how much would the set cost? How large is such a set?

2. If you check out a book from the public library and do not return it, what laws have you broken? How may you be punished?

3. It bothers you that one of your local police officers keeps parking his police car in a no-parking zone every time he stops for a cup of coffee. One day you tell him he is setting a bad example for the community. He replies that it is his right as a law officer. What laws (if any) has he broken? Can he give you a hard time for criticizing him?

4. You and two friends see a purse snatcher grab an elderly woman's pocketbook. You grab him as he runs by. Instantly, he fights back. You and your two friends work him over and hold him for the police. What sort of trouble might the three of you be in?

5. Just for the fun of it, you and a friend sneak into the local theater without paying admission. What possible legal trouble can come your way?

6. One day you decide to go skiing instead of attending school. What is the worst thing that can legally happen to you?

7. Even though you know the city does not allow you to ride a bike on the sidewalks, you do so anyway. One evening, just before dark, you run into a little old lady carrying her shopping bag. The ambulance driver tells you her leg is broken. How much trouble are you in?

8. You and your girlfriend go out for the evening even though her father told her not to. When you walk her to the door, her dad dashes out and tells you he is going to have you arrested for criminal trespass. Will the charge hold?

9. You and your brother decide to raise registered dogs to make some money. You have exactly eleven puppies in your basement when the dog control officer knocks on the door. The city code says that no person may have more than two dogs without a kennel license. You don't have such a license. What do you do now?

10. You are test-driving a motorcycle you saw advertised in the Sunday paper. It runs like a dream until you lose control on a corner and pile it up. The owner calls the police. Are you in legal trouble?

11. Just for the fun of it, you and a couple of friends plug up the toilets and sinks in the rest room of a downtown store. The place is just beginning to look like Niagara Falls when a store security officer nails you. What sort of trouble are you in at this point?

Some of the foregoing questions should have been pretty easy to answer. For a few, you may have discovered that there was no straightforward answer. This is because many things have to be considered where the law is concerned. Later on, you will get a chance to look closely at some cases involving young people. The practice you just had in finding answers to legal questions should help you find answers to these later questions.

7. I Am More Important than They Are— Or Am I?

Laws are made to protect the rights of people and to help people live together in an orderly manner. In order to accomplish this, certain restrictions are put on the acts of people so that the rights of others may be respected. A famous judge on the U.S. Supreme Court once summed up this problem when he said: "The right to swing your arm stops just at the point of another man's chin."

By setting limits on what you may do, the law gives you freedom. So long as you stay within the limits set, you are free to act. Knowing that you must not do anything outside those limits adds to your freedom because there is no question of how far you may go. Imagine what your life would be like if you did not know any rules. If all you knew was that rules existed and that you would be punished if you broke them, your life would be filled with uncertainty. You would never know what was safe from punishment until you tried it. You may think a rule is unfair. Yet, so long as you obey the rule, you are safe from punishment. If the only way to learn the rule is by breaking it, you have no security at all. When you know the rules, you don't have to worry about them.

Another question has to be considered concerning the protection of rights and the giving of freedom. It was what the Supreme Court justice was thinking about when he spoke of arm swinging. At what point do one person's actions begin to infringe on the rights of others? When does the exercise of personal freedom begin to threaten the freedom of the group? In other words, at what point does the other man's chin appear?

Lawmakers and courts face this problem every day. How can the rights of the individual be protected without taking away the rights of society as a group? How can groups of people be given the greatest amount of freedom without letting individuals take advantage of those around them? This is one of the most difficult questions in modern law. It is also one of the most vital points of law as far as you are concerned, both as a person and as a member of society.

Our Bill of Rights attempts to guard the rights of the nation's people from too much government. Yet society cannot allow a few individuals to harm the group by demanding individual rights that are unreasonable. Of course, what was reasonable a hundred years ago may not be reasonable today.

Many court decisions have dealt with questions of individual versus group rights. Countless lawmakers have struggled with the problem as they tried to write laws that were good both for individuals and for society. The results of court decisions and lawmakers' work have, at times, been less than successful. As society becomes more complicated, the job gets more difficult.

EXERCISES	• To better understand the problems facing the law where individual and group rights are concerned, read the following situations. Discuss them as a class. Try to reach a decision as to what is proper in each situation. After you have reached a decision (or have failed to do so), consider the same problem in terms of a hundred years ago. Then consider it fifty years into the future. How does the passage of time affect your thinking?

1. Mike had looked at the old oak tree for quite some time. It was dying and dangerous and had to be cut down. When Mike found out what it would cost to have a tree service remove the tree, he decided to do it himself. Then Mike learned that he had to buy a permit to remove the tree. Before the permit could be issued, a city forester had to inspect the old oak. Worse than that, Mike had to buy a tree-trimmer's license to do the work. To get the license, he had to get a bonding company to guarantee he wouldn't harm any property, public or private, in removing the tree. Finally, he would have to plant a new tree where the old one stood.

2. Lonny worked hard to make a living for his wife and two children. All that Lonny asked for out of life was a chance to enjoy his family and to be left alone by others. He seldom got involved in or excited by things that went on around him. "Live and let live" was his motto. Almost by accident, Lonny got into the repair business as a sideline. Soon he found he could earn as much on evenings and on weekends as he did from his regular job. Lonny converted his garage into a repair shop. Since he worked evenings, many customers arrived late with work for him. One Thursday night, a police officer entered the repair shop. He told Lonny the area was not zoned for business and that the shop had not been given the necessary fire inspection. Lonny was out of business a minute later.

3. When cheerleader tryouts were announced, Evelyn was the first to sign up. She wanted to be a cheerleader more than she ever wanted anything. From the first practice session, everyone knew that Evelyn was the best. For the first time in months, Evelyn felt good about herself. She had been having trouble in school all year with students and teachers alike. Now she was making up for it. After the final practice session came the actual tryout. Evelyn won it hands down. It was the happiest moment of her life. The next day a questionnaire was sent to the Student Council. Each cheerleader contestant was listed. The council members were asked to rate them on the basis of citizenship, school spirit, sportsmanship, and whether they should represent the school. Evelyn scored lowest of the twenty-six girls who tried out.

4. The little town of Josten seemed to be withering away. Its young people moved away when they were old enough, and new people never seemed to stop in town long enough to settle there. Everyone knew the town needed industry to survive. One day the Chamber of Commerce announced that an industry was coming to Josten. It would hire more than 300 local workers. Overnight, the town's future looked brighter than it had in years. For weeks the new industry was all anyone talked about. Then the townspeople found something else to discuss. The new plant needed room, lots of it. It also had to have the rail spur and highway near it. Only one area was suitable. Every landowner except one was willing to sell land for the new plant. The lone holdout was seventy-eight years old. His grandfather had homesteaded the land on which his home now stood. No matter what he was offered or how carefully the situation was explained, the old fellow refused to listen. "I was born on this land. I might as well die on it," he declared. Many of the townspeople thought that was a good idea and suggested that he do his dying soon. Others decided to get the courts to force him to leave his land.

8. "But I Am Only a Child, Officer"

The law makes a distinction between juvenile and adult lawbreakers. This distinction has both good and bad points. For many years, our juvenile laws were based on English common-law decisions. Under this type of law, a child under the age of seven was considered unable to commit a crime. A child over the age of four-teen was considered an adult and was tried accordingly. Between the ages of seven and fourteen, a juvenile was said to be incapable of crime. However, if the court felt that a juvenile understood the difference between right and wrong, he was tried as an adult. In this way, many children under the age of fourteen were given death sentences for things they did.

The first juvenile reformatories or juvenile correction homes in the United States were built in the 1820's. This was our first real step in caring for juvenile lawbreakers. It wasn't until 1899 that the nation's first juvenile court was started in Chicago. From then on, as the idea of juvenile courts spread to other cities and states, juvenile offenders have been treated differently from adults.

This has not always been to their advantage. Until the past few years, juveniles suspected of breaking the law often did not have the same rights as adults. Before then, children could be held in juvenile detention homes without a chance to talk with lawyers or have bond set so they could go home. Juveniles didn't have trials; they had *hearings*. For years, juveniles stood before a judge without a lawyer. Often, neither they nor their parents knew they were allowed to have a lawyer represent them at their hearings. Children often were given sentences of several years in state reformatories for misdemeanors that would have sent an adult to the county jail or another *penal institution* for a month.

In recent years, many states have tried hard to overcome such accidental injustices to juvenile lawbreakers. Some of this change has been effected by Supreme Court decisions. Much of the change has come because people felt a need to prevent young people from getting into more trouble rather than punish them for what they already did.

Generally, now, juvenile lawbreakers are not booked by police. If possible, they are released into the care of their parents instead of held in jail. When they are brought to court, it is to a special juvenile court where hearings are not open to the public. Names of young lawbreak-

ers usually are not printed in the newspapers. Exceptions are made when youthful offenders are charged with crimes such as murder. In major felonies involving loss of life, or especially terrible assaults, it is common to identify the accused once the district attorney decides to bring them to trial. Even if found guilty, children and youths often are allowed to remain at home on probation—as long as they do not get into trouble again. If the home situation seems bad for the child, he or she may be sent to live with a relative or put in a foster home. At times, the young lawbreaker is sent to a facility for delinquent youth.

In many states special juvenile prisons have been and are being built to house youthful offenders. One reason for this is the vast number of youth charged with serious crimes. There is no question that housing young offenders with adult criminals is a poor idea. Juvenile prisons are an effort to provide for those serious younger offenders who are considered beyond the control of less formal facilities, while keeping them away from the direct influence of older criminals.

Another method of accomplishing this same goal is to add special juvenile wings to adult prisons. Gaining acceptance in some areas are facilities sometimes referred to as youth boot camps. These boot camps are run in the style of basic-training facilities for the military. They are designed to give young, usually first-time offenders, a taste of what life is like when they lose many of the freedoms they take for granted.

Youth boot camps provide strict supervision, require lots of physical effort, and demand that the young offenders follow orders instantly and without protest. Those who successfully complete their assigned time in such a boot camp are free to return to society. Those who are unable or unwilling to accept the demands imposed by the camp leaders are generally sent immediately to a prison or other detention facility.

Whether the boot camp approach will prove successful over the long haul is as yet undecided. Some states have experienced considerable success with this concept. Others have been disappointed with the results.

All of these measures are intended to steer the young offender away from more crime. Putting young people in prison with older criminals will just make them more likely to become criminals themselves.

Some states have even gone a step further and passed special sets of laws called *juvenile codes.* These codes are a special way of considering the law when the offender is under the age of eighteen. They are another step in trying to keep youth from having criminal records and perhaps becoming hardened criminals. Social workers, rather than police, often work with young lawbreakers. Even police departments hire special juvenile officers, just as the courts have juvenile probation officers and judges.

Many youths and adults have taken advantage of the system. Some young people have committed crime after crime, knowing they are likely to be treated less harshly than an adult who does the same things. Adults have enlisted young people to commit crimes for them, or to help them in criminal acts. The idea is that young lawbreakers have far less chance of being severely punished than do adults. Probably the most striking example of this is the rapidly growing number of juvenile "hit men." These youthful killers are hired to commit murders. Both the killers and those who hire them are aware that juvenile codes and courts are likely to give the young offenders easier sentences than would be the case with adult killers. In the illegal drug trade, preteens are often used as runners for dealers, for many of the same reasons.

As more and more extremely young criminals emerge in society, the public has demanded increasingly harsh measures to stem the tide of criminal activity among youths.

One result of having more serious crimes committed by children and youths is that some district attorneys try youthful offenders as adults. It is not uncommon to have a youth of sixteen or seventeen tried as an adult in cases of brutal assaults, rapes, and homicides.

In the authors' home state, effective in 1996, the state legislature voted to allow children as young as twelve to be tried as adults in cases involving major felonies. The fact that the state's governor, a man known for his liberal policies and desire to protect children, signed the bill indicates the gravity of the growing problem of serious youthful offenders.

At the same time, in the same state, a ten-year-old boy was accused of having brutally murdered an eighteen-month-old infant. Under state law that boy cannot be tried for the crime and cannot be sent to prison. He is considered too young to be fully capable of understanding the crime.

In another state during 1996, a child of six was involved in the killing of another child. The six-year-old did not even have to appear in court. State law assumes a child six years of age is not capable of committing a crime.

Society tries to protect children and youths when they make bad choices. At the same time, members of society feel that children and youths should be held accountable for criminal actions, even if they should also be treated differently from adults. Their arrest, their court appearance, and their punishment if found guilty should not be handled the same way. Obviously, however, society may have to do something to keep willful lawbreakers from taking advantage of the juvenile codes.

| **EXERCISES** | • Since you can't watch a juvenile court in action, the next best thing might be to bring the court to you. Your teacher can arrange to have a juvenile court judge visit your class to explain the workings of the court and answer your questions concerning the court.
• As a group, prepare a list of questions you would like the juvenile judge to answer during his or her visit with you. Here are a few questions you might include: |

1. What is the maximum age for defendants in juvenile court?

2. Under what circumstances might a minor be tried outside the juvenile court?

3. What services does the court offer to offenders and their families in an effort to keep young lawbreakers from getting into further difficulties with the law?

4. What are the possible sentences a juvenile court judge can impose? What are the various correctional institutions to which young offenders may be sent in your area? How do these operate?

5. When might a juvenile court judge order a child to be removed from his or her own home?

6. What does it cost the taxpayers to provide a year's care for a young offender in the various state and county institutions?

7. How successful are the court's attempts to keep first offenders from getting into further trouble?

8. What is an actual juvenile court hearing like?

9. How do juvenile police and court records differ from those of adults?

- After your class has met with a juvenile judge, you will want to discuss what you learned. Decide how well the juvenile court program seems to be working. You may also have some ideas that might improve the success of the juvenile courts.

- Use the information the judge gives you about correctional institutions as a starting point and learn more about your area's correctional and penal institutions. You may want to write the various institutions to find out where people found guilty of various crimes are sent and the ages of inmates sent there. Also, try to learn as much as possible about places such as "halfway houses" and the like, which often deal exclusively with youths.

- The situations that follow are to be read and discussed as a class. Try to decide whether the juvenile in each case should be treated as a juvenile or whether there might be cause to treat the offender as an adult.

---

1. Tom's father had whipped him five times that week. His mother had just locked him in his room for the third time in a week. The six-year-old felt that his parents no longer loved him. He felt around in his pocket for the book of matches he had stolen from his uncle the night before. He set fire to his bedroom curtains. The firefighters rescued Tom from his room. His baby sister burned to death in her crib.

2. Bob wanted a car of his own more than anything else in the world. At seventeen, he was the only guy in his gang who did not own one. Bob had taken driver education and had a driver's license. All he lacked was a car. Because his mother was on welfare and Bob didn't have a job, he couldn't see any way of buying a car. So, night after night, Bob picked up cars from parking lots and private garages and went "joyriding." Twice he was picked up, but each time the court had released him to his mother. This time he had been really unlucky. Not only had he been picked up, but he had run over a small child while trying to get away from the police.

3. Sally wasn't a criminal. All she did was pick up small items from store counters without paying for them. It wasn't that she really needed what she took. Most thirteen-year-old girls don't have much use for twenty-nine tubes of lipstick. It was the thrill of getting away with it that kept Sally going from store to store, picking up items that caught her eye. When Sally was first caught by a store detective, her mother paid for the items and that was it. The second time, Sally had to go to the police station. This time it looked as though Sally might have to appear at a juvenile hearing.

4. Fred had little use for anything or anybody weaker than he. For this reason, he loved to hurt dogs and cats. When he was eleven or twelve, his teachers and parents thought it was something Fred would outgrow. But, at sixteen, not only did he still torture small animals to death every chance he got, but he was always thinking of new and more painful ways to bring about death to his victims. When an angry neighbor filed charges

against Fred for torturing the neighbor's puppy to death, Fred's parents were outraged. "He is just a boy who is curious about things!" they protested angrily. "Freddy isn't some sort of criminal. He is our baby."

5. Linda's father kept a loaded .38 in the top drawer of his bedside table. The entire family knew the weapon was there. They knew it was bought because of the growing crime rate in their city. Linda and her younger brothers were told time and time again to leave the weapon alone. One day, Linda mentioned the .38 to some friends, who asked to see it. Since her parents were both at work and she was not likely to get caught, Linda brought the revolver out for the others to see. In the course of looking at it, fifteen-year-old Janice accidentally shot Martha to death.

6. As a senior in high school, Jill was four feet ten inches tall and weighed eighty-seven pounds. She said little. Her silence and small size went with her young-looking face to give her something of a doll-like appearance. When she began dating Ralph, the team's fullback, her parents and friends teased Jill good naturedly. "Beauty and the Beast," their friends nicknamed the pair. When Ralph gave Jill his ring, she had to wear it on a chain around her neck. When Ralph later asked for his ring back, Jill didn't bat an eye. She handed him the ring, smiled her little smile, and went into the house. Two days later, she met Ralph in the school corridor. Once more she smiled. Jill was still smiling as she stuck an ice pick into Ralph's stomach.

9. What If You Are Arrested?

Being taken into police custody is no fun. It can be frightening, embarrassing, and may result in a change of lifestyle for quite some time. However, there are certain protections for an individual who is arrested. They apply whether that person is guilty or not.

To begin with, an arrested person must be informed of the charge(s) against him. Under certain circumstances, this charge may not be made the minute he is brought to the police station. No one, though, can be held in *legal custody* for any great length of time without

being formally charged and told of the charge. Once a person is told of the charge against him, he can start preparing his defense.

Other than to correctly identify himself by giving his name and address, an arrested person does not need to talk with officers or give information to them. This protection comes from the Fifth Amendment to the Constitution, which says that no person accused of a crime can be forced to say something that might incriminate him. Going further than the Bill of Rights was the famous *Miranda* case, in which the Supreme Court said an arrested person must be told of his right to remain silent and to consult a lawyer. As a result of this famous court decision, arrested persons are told of their rights before questioning. A statement similar to the following is read to an arrested person before he is officially questioned:

You have the right to remain silent. Anything you say can and may be used against you in a court of law. You have the right to talk to a lawyer and have him with you while you are being questioned. If you cannot afford to hire a lawyer, one will be appointed to represent you before any questioning, if you wish one. If you decide to answer questions now without a lawyer present, you will have the right to stop answering at any time. You also have the right to stop answering at any time until you talk to a lawyer.

This statement is a bit different in its wording from the one you usually hear on TV. This is because the Supreme Court did not state exactly what an arrested person must be told. It said a person who has been arrested must be told of his right to an attorney and that anything he says may be used in court to help convict him. It is up to the local police department to make this clear. For this reason, many police departments use different words in an effort to correctly inform a suspect of his rights. Many police departments use a special set of instructions for young people placed under arrest. This is an attempt to make sure the juvenile knows exactly what is being said to him about his rights to legal help.

An arrested person is allowed "one phone call," which we all know about from watching television. This means that he may contact either his family or his lawyer to tell them where he is and let them know he needs help. This call does not have to be allowed the instant a prisoner enters the police station.

If an individual cannot afford to hire his own lawyer, one will be hired for him. This is because the law says everyone, rich or poor, is entitled to be defended by a lawyer. This used to be taken to mean that defense had to take place at a trial. Now the courts say that defense begins at the time of arrest. No one, no matter what crime he is accused of, has to answer any questions without having a lawyer with him at the time of questioning.

Those accused of crimes are often offered the opportunity to take advantage of plea bargaining. A plea bargain involves pleading guilty to a lesser offense than the one to which the person is charged. Or, if there are several offenses involved, a plea bargain may consist of pleading guilty to one or perhaps several of the multiple charges.

By pleading guilty, the defendant avoids having to go to trial. Since he or she is pleading guilty to a lesser charge or to fewer charges, the resulting sentence is less than would be the case if the accused is found guilty following a trial. Of course, by accepting a plea bargain, the accused is pleading guilty to a crime and stands no chance of being found innocent by a jury.

Victims of crimes and their families quite often resent the fact that the defendant is allowed to plea bargain and escape maximum punishment. So why do prosecutors accept plea bargains? Often, even though the prosecutors are certain of the guilt of the accused, they fear they lack evidence that will convince jury members to find the defendant guilty. In such cases the prosecutor would rather have the criminal punished somewhat than to escape punishment totally.

Perhaps more often, an accused is offered a plea bargain or even immunity from prosecution in return for testimony against another individual the prosecutor feels is even more dangerous. Thus, someone accused of a felony may totally escape prosecution because he or she is willing to testify against a second individual who is guilty of a greater crime.

Plea bargaining can be an effective tool for lawyers to use to help their clients escape prosecution or receive lighter sentences.

While a prisoner is waiting for trial, she has the right to ask for *bail*. Unless a person is accused of an especially severe crime, such as murder or kidnapping, she is entitled to leave jail until she is found guilty at a formal trial. In order to help preserve the rights of an arrested person, a special paper called a writ of *habeas corpus* is sometimes used. This is obtained by a lawyer from the courts when the police or other law enforcement people are holding a prisoner without properly charging him or allowing bail to be made. This legal act keeps people from being locked up in jail for weeks or even months without ever being legally charged.

EXERCISES	• Before moving on, let's discuss some questions about being arrested. You will probably think of other questions while discussing these. When you do, ask about them. You may also have to do some outside reading or research to find the answers.

1. What could you do, personally, if you were held in city jail without being charged?
2. If the local police refused to allow you to contact your family or a lawyer, what could you do about it?
3. How could you prove to a court that you had not been informed of your rights if two police officers said you had been?
4. The statement of rights given as an example did not ask whether you understood your rights. On TV, the police usually ask the suspect whether he understands his rights as read to him. What would happen if a suspect said, "No, I do not understand my rights"?
5. Many people are granted the right to get out of jail by posting bail. What happens when a person has that right but has no money with which to "make" bail?
6. Suppose you have a lawyer appointed to represent you and you don't like the person. Can you ask for another lawyer?
7. When a lawyer is appointed for a person who can't afford one, who pays for the lawyer's fees?

The actual process of being arrested is a lot different from what you see on television. Short of going through the process of arrest, questioning, and booking yourself, the best way to learn about it is to talk to someone who has gone the route. Since students who have already had the experience may feel uncomfortable about describing the process, you and two or three classmates might make a project of contacting the local police and discovering the physical procedure of arrest. Most local police stations are more than willing to explain the procedure if you just call ahead and make an appointment. Explain that it is part of a class project. Then the group involved can share their findings with the rest of the class.

• Here are some questions you may ask. They will help you and your group think of other questions. Remember to find out how an adult might be treated differently from a juvenile when brought to the police station and accused of a crime.

1. What do arresting officers consider "reasonable or justifiable force" in arresting a suspect?
2. How can a suspect under the influence of drugs or alcohol be given her rights? If she can't, how long may she be held without contacting her family or lawyer?
3. What is the procedure after a suspect enters the police station?
4. What is *booking,* and how is it done?
5. When are a minor's parents notified by the police?
6. Can a minor demand that her parents not be notified of her arrest?
7. How long can a person be held without being charged? Does this hold true for a juvenile as well?
8. May a police officer ask for "information" without reading a suspect her rights?
9. How long may an arrested person be questioned without food or rest? Does this time change if the person is a juvenile?
10. Can a lawyer force officers to stop questioning an arrested person?
11. What happens if an arrested person cannot locate either her family or her attorney by phone?
12. Are juveniles put in the same cells as older persons in city jail?

13. Is everyone given a jail uniform? Are belts and shoelaces taken away from prisoners?

14. What if an arrested person claims she is ill and needs a doctor? Can she ask for her family doctor?

15. If a person does not post bail, how long can she be held in jail?

16. How often are prisoners in a city or county jail injured by other prisoners?

10. Your Rights in Court

We have looked at your basic rights at the time of arrest. If you are brought to trial, you have a number of rights and rules of justice that protect you during your trial. These same rules of justice give you certain protections before and after your trial as well.

One of our most important rights under the law is the *separation of powers*. This means that the person or agency arresting you cannot try you. Nor can that person decide upon your punishment if you are found guilty. Without this right, none of those that follow would be of much use to an accused person.

One of our most basic ideas of justice is that the accused person is *presumed to be innocent until proven guilty*. If you are brought to trial you are not supposed to have to prove your innocence. It's the prosecution's job to prove the defendant guilty. If the prosecution cannot do so, then you are supposed to be considered innocent of the crime and found not guilty.

Another protection for the person accused of a crime is the right to a *public trial*. This trial is supposed to come fairly soon after charges are made against the suspect. Having a public trial is meant to keep law enforcement agencies and courts from concealing what they are doing from the rest of the people. Everything said at a trial is supposed to be recorded so lawyers may later check these statements for errors or lies that might have harmed a client. Having the trial within a reasonable length of time keeps the state from postponing it until important witnesses have died, moved, or even forgotten what they said and did.

All persons brought to trial are allowed to request a *trial by jury*. A group of people chosen by the court will listen to the evidence and the defense. Then they decide upon the guilt or innocence of the person on trial. People who serve on juries are supposed to have no personal interest in the case and to have no opinions about the case before serving on the jury. Although some people say that jury trials aren't always the best way to decide a case, the right to demand a jury does help protect the rights of a person accused of a crime. It is one way of forcing the prosecution to prove that the person on trial really is guilty.

An accused person may be certain someone knows things about the case that would help him. Sometimes witnesses do not want to testify. Perhaps they are afraid. Maybe they just don't want to "get involved." Whatever the reason, an accused person can force such witnesses to come into court and tell what they know or saw. This is called the *power of subpoena*. A *subpoena* is a court order that requires a witness to testify in a trial. Without this right, many accused people might not be able to get certain witnesses to appear in court.

Once a public trial is actually under way, an accused person has the right to confront each and every witness who says things against him. No witness may make secret statements to the court. The accused has the right to listen to what witnesses say—to actually see and hear them make their statements. When these statements have been made, the accused person's lawyer may then *cross-examine* these witnesses. The lawyer may ask questions that the witnesses must answer. It allows the defendant's lawyer to attempt to show that the testimony given isn't correct or does not mean what the prosecution says it does. In this way, the person accused of a crime may keep witnesses from making untrue charges and getting away with it.

Perhaps the most important single protection an accused person has is that he can't be forced to testify against himself. Just as when a person is arrested, a person on trial cannot be made to say things that might help to prove him guilty. We call this *freedom from self-incrimination.* This does not mean that a person on trial cannot testify. If he and his lawyer believe that it is a good idea for him to tell his side to the court, he may do so. Once a person on trial does allow himself to become a witness he may be cross-examined by the prosecution. If things come out that hurt his case, he cannot stop them from being used against him.

Law officers are allowed to search the scene of a crime for evidence. When such evidence is found, they may use it in court against the accused person. Under certain conditions, the home and business of an accused person may be searched for more evidence. There are limits to how much searching law officers can do and when they can do it. If the accused or his lawyer can show that the police were unreasonable in their searching and gathering of evidence, that evidence cannot be used at the trial.

In the event that you are found to be not guilty of the crime for which you are tried, the prosecution cannot bring you to trial again for the same offense. This is an extremely important safeguard for your rights in court. Were it not for this rule of justice, you could be found innocent and then be arrested for the same crime before you got out of the courtroom. In that way, you might have to stand trial a number of times for something you did not do.

Although you can't be forced to come to trial a second time if you are found innocent, you can appeal the court's decision if you are found guilty. This gives you a second chance to prove you are not guilty in some cases. Your lawyer can go to a higher court and ask that the case be tried again. If the lawyer can show that there was something wrong with the first trial or there were errors in testimony or if new evidence has been found, you may be given a new trial. If you are found innocent at the new trial, you are free.

There are several protections that help you after you have been convicted of a crime. One of these keeps the government from taking property and possessions from the family of a person who has committed a crime. Though this protection has been with us since the signing of the Constitution, two major exceptions have come into being in recent years.

The first of these exceptions is that governments at all levels have been allowed to seize property used in the illegal drug trade. Thus cars, boats, and buildings have been taken by the government when these items were found to have been used by drug dealers. In addition, property purchased with profits from the drug trade can also be seized and kept by the government. If profits from drug deals were used to buy a home, a business, gifts, etc., all these can be seized by the government. The fact that members of the family of the convicted individual live in the home, work in the business, or accepted the gifts makes no difference.

A second exception to protection from seizure comes when the Internal Revenue Service determines that tax evasion has taken place. In many instances bank accounts, autos, homes, and even businesses have been seized by the IRS to cover payment of back taxes. At times these bank accounts and other possessions were owned jointly by the accused and someone else or even owned entirely by another family member.

Another constitutional protection for those convicted of a crime is that they may not be punished in a cruel or unusual way. Such punishments as branding, cutting off a person's hand, blinding, starving, and the like are not allowed. From time to time an attorney tries to prove that locking a person up in prison is cruel punishment. Convicts have been known to file suit claiming that having to eat jail or prison food or not getting to watch their favorite TV program constitutes cruel punishment. Such appeals seldom go far in the courts.

EXERCISES	• Below are some questions to talk about concerning the rights and protections of people who are brought to trial for crimes. You will probably have questions and ideas of your own to discuss as well.

1. Don't people often assume that if the police have brought a person to trial, he or she must be guilty? What does this do to the idea that a person is innocent until he or she is proven guilty?

2. Every person accused of having committed a crime has the right to have a trial before a jury. Should this also include such things as traffic offenses? What about a juvenile who appears in juvenile court, where the hearing is closed to the public and no jury is present?

3. If a person is seen actually committing a crime, why should time and money be wasted on a trial that might last for several days?

4. Why might some people say that a jury trial is not always the best sort of trial?

5. Some people do not want to become involved as witnesses in a court trial. Even though such a person has information that might help the person on trial, couldn't a subpoena make the witness angry enough to lie in court?

6. Are there any times when it might be a good idea to allow witnesses to appear before a court in disguise? When might the court decide to let someone testify without letting the accused know who that person was?

7. What might be an example of unreasonable searching done by a law enforcement group?

8. What was the thinking of the lawmakers when they said a person could not be forced to stand trial twice for the same crime but could ask for a second trial if found guilty?

9. If a traffic court judge forced a drunk driver to spend several evenings with ambulance drivers, picking up traffic victims, would that be a cruel and unusual punishment?

Just as being arrested is the best way to learn about arrest, so is being on trial the best way to learn how a court trial really works. However, that is a painful way to gain knowledge. Sitting in on an actual court trial can tell you a lot about the workings of a court and help explain the rights and rules of justice just discussed. A group of students with an adult might plan to attend a court trial and report their findings to the class.

Your teacher can contact a judge to learn when a jury trial is being held that would be of interest to your class. So long as you do nothing to interfere with the trial, you will be allowed to watch a court trial in progress. This is one of our safeguards. You are the public, and the public is allowed to watch trials in progress.

> • Here are a few things you should watch for while attending a trial:

1. How are members of the jury selected from those called as possible jury members?
2. What sorts of reasons do attorneys have for dismissing prospective jurors from the jury?
3. How many people in the courtroom help conduct the trial? What are their jobs?
4. What special ways of talking do lawyers have during a trial?
5. What are some things that happen during the trial that cause it to take a lot of time?
6. For what reasons are the members of the jury sent out of the courtroom from time to time?
7. What part does the defendant play during the trial?
8. What happened during the trial to make you think that the accused either got a fair trial or an unfair one?

Review Quiz II

A. Sentence Completions

> **Directions:** Supply the word that correctly completes each of the following statements.

1. _____ of the law is not considered a valid excuse for break-ing the law.

2. Using laws to set limits on actions may actually give people _____ because they know how far they may go without getting into trouble.

3. Laws provide for the protection of personal _____ and freedoms.

4. Laws and courts must often consider the rights of the _____ as related to the rights of the group.

5. A prison may also be called a _____ institution.

6. The _____ Amendment gives a person the right to refuse to answer questions which might incriminate him or her.

7. When a person is arrested, he or she is said to have been taken into legal

   _____ .

8. A person accused of a crime is presumed to be _____ until proven guilty.

9. A legal safeguard guaranteed all citizens accused of crimes is the right to a public

   _____ .

10. Another constitutional protection for those accused of wrongdoing is the right to a trial by _____ .

B. Definitions

Directions: Choose from the list the word or term that best matches each definition. Write the word or term selected in the space before the definition it matches. Some words in the list will not be used.

arrest	cross-examine	juvenile codes	subpoena
bail	evidence	Miranda	suspect
Bailey	habeas corpus	offender	witness
Bill of Rights	hearing	precedent	
crime	juvenile	self-incrimination	

11. _____ This previous court decision has a bearing on a current case.

12. _____ This document was created over two hundred years go to protect the people of our nation from too much government power.

13. _____ A person too young to be legally considered an adult is called this.

14. _____ This is a court appearance for a young offender.

15. _____ These are special sets of laws that apply to minors in some states.

16. _____ A person who has broken the law may be referred to by this name.

17. _____ This is to take a person into custody of the law.

18. _____ This famous court ruling says that those accused of a crime must be informed of their rights before questioning.

19. _____ This is a pledge of money or property that allows a person to leave jail while awaiting trial.

20. _____ A person thought to be guilty, or possibly guilty, of a crime is called this.

21. _____ This writ or document keeps police from illegally holding a person in jail.

22. _____ This power gives an accused person the right to require a witness to testify in court.

23. _____ Police search for this in attempting to solve a crime or prove guilt.

24. _____ This is something an accused person says that helps to prove he or she is guilty.

25. _____ During a trial, lawyers are allowed to do this to verify statements made by witnesses.

Part II

How the Law Applies to Us

Introduction

Now that you have read and discussed the first part of *You and the Law,* you should know more about what the law hopes to accomplish. You also should be aware that every person has certain rights and obligations under the law. It is only as we understand both our rights and our duties that we can receive the full benefit of the law.

The second part of *You and the Law* contains a number of short sections. Each section deals with a type of legal problem that individuals your age may encounter. Obviously, most of us want to avoid these problems. Many of them are a lot easier to get into than to get out of. Quite a number are what the authors call "accidental" situations. By this we mean things that happen to people without any real planning. When two fellows get into a fight over a ball game and one ends up in the hospital while the other is in juvenile court, it is an "accidental" violation of the law. Neither intended things to go as far as they did, and both suffered. Thankfully, the law does take into account "accidental" happenings.

Each situation in this part of *You and the Law* gives you questions to answer. You can find some of the answers in the first part of the book or in the glossary at the end. Others you may be able to answer through discussion or your own experience. Some questions will require you to do further reading. Whenever you have a chance, actually look up what the law says for your state, county, or city.

The more you learn about the law, the less likely you are to feel that the law is a monster that can't be understood. Also, the better will be your opportunity for protection and help under the law.

11. Taking the Law into Your Own Hands or Protecting Your Rights

A hundred and more years ago, miners, ranchers, and other western settlers often had to provide their own protection under the law. This resulted in a rough-and-ready way of life that never completely disappeared from many parts of western America. This spirit of taking care of oneself became so much a part of American thought that today many people still try to settle matters themselves first rather than call for outside help.

Such independence is both good and bad.

Countless news items tell of people refusing to aid others or even to report crimes in progress. Millions of readers become upset at such articles and remark, "If I'd been there, things would have been different." For example, a news report told of a group of women who attacked a rapist with knives. The local police arrested the women involved in the attack. It was a matter for the law, the police said, and citizens can't be allowed to take the law into their own hands.

QUESTIONS

1. Just exactly what is the difference between taking the law into your own hands and standing up for your rights or for the rights of others?

_____

_____

2. School personnel and parents are often guilty of confusing students in this matter. How many times have teachers and parents told children to "stop being a tattletale and settle your own problems" and then gotten angry when the children *did* settle their own difficulties? At what point should we settle our own difficulties, and when should we call for help from the law?

(a) Give an example of a situation in which you or your friends took the law into your own hands and the matter was settled without difficulty. Don't identify the people involved.

_____

_____

(b) Now give an instance in which you or others relied on yourselves and it turned out badly. Again, don't identify the people involved.

_____

_____

3. It is generally considered proper for people to defend themselves, their families, and their property from harm. Give some possible instances in which you or your family would be justified in taking the law into your own hands in defense of family or property.

_____

_____

4. In defending oneself or one's property, the question is exactly how much defense is proper. In each of the following situations, decide what is or is not justified, and suggest alternative solutions to each problem. If there are no other solutions, give the reasons why.

   (a) The neighbor's boy is beating up your little sister. To teach him a lesson and to protect her, you beat him up.

_____

_____

   (b) It is night and you hear a prowler. He has opened the window and stuck his head into the living room. You hit him soundly over the head with a baseball bat you are carrying.

_____

_____

   (c) You and your friends are walking home from a night ball game when you hear screams from an alley. A man is attacking a woman who is screaming for help. When you approach, the man turns on you with a knife. Two of the guys go for him with boards they found lying in the alley. You all jump in to help.

_____

_____

   (d) Your mother is driving you someplace when her car gets a fender bender. The other driver jumps out of his car and is coming toward your mother with a mean look and clenched fists.

_____

_____

5. The ultimate in defense of people or property comes when someone takes the life of an intruder or attacker. Self-defense has long been recognized as a valid legal defense in certain instances. Only a hundred years ago in the American West, it was considered self-defense when one man killed another during an argument so long as both men were armed. The current thinking is that killing another in defense of one's own life or the lives of others may, at times, be justified. It is almost never considered legally acceptable to take a person's life when only property is involved.

When Colorado's legislature passed the "Make My Day" law, there was considerable comment raised throughout the nation. The term "Make My Day" came from a line in a Clint Eastwood movie, by the way. Colorado's "Make My Day" law says that a citizen fearing extreme bodily harm or death is allowed to protect himself or herself, as well as other people. If this protection results in the death of the attacker, the one defending himself, herself, or others is innocent of causing wrongful death.

However, there are certain conditions under which this law operates. The law states that the person defending against attack normally must be on his or her own property. Further, it pretty generally requires that the defender must be inside his or her own house and the attacker must have entered the home. At least the attacker must be attempting to make a violent entry, such as kicking down the door or coming in through a window he or she has just broken.

This law has resulted in very little loss of life. Only a handful of Colorado residents have killed someone invading their home.

You have done a lot of thinking, discussing, and writing on the subject of taking the law into your own hands. How does the "Make My Day" law fit into what you know about our laws and how laws are intended to enable us to live together in society?

_____

_____

6. Finish this section by writing a statement in which you explain just how far you may go when it comes to taking the law into your own hands.

_____

_____

_____

12. Failure to Obey the Police

A great many of us know the sick feeling that comes over us when we run into trouble. A normal reaction to trouble is to run away. Running doesn't change things, though. The broken window is still broken, and the mangled fender is still a mess. No matter how far we run, we still end up either paying for the mess we made or living in fear every time the doorbell or phone rings.

QUESTIONS

1. Our laws are set up to discourage people from running away or from not obeying the police. For example, what is the penalty for having a traffic accident?

_____

_____

2. What is the penalty for having the same accident but leaving the scene of the accident without

reporting it? _____

_____

3. If running away from trouble is basic to human nature, so is resentment of authority. Lots of us hate to be "ordered around," whether by police, teachers, parents, or any other authority figures. The urge to disobey is strong in many of us. People often resist arrest. What are the most likely reasons for resisting arrest?

_____

_____

_____

4. We have read of young suspects who were running from the police and in the process were shot to death. Why should the police be allowed to fire at fleeing suspects?

_____

_____

5. What is wrong with allowing officers to fire at youths who are running away from them?

_____

_____

6. Another form of resisting authority is name-calling. Why do people openly challenge police officers by name-calling, fist shaking, and other such acts?

_____

_____

7. What is it about certain police officers that causes even law-abiding citizens to resent them and feel like challenging their authority?

_____

_____

_____

13. Unlawful Assembly, Rioting, and Looting

We have all seen enough TV news reports to have some idea of the total disaster that can be caused by riots. The destruction of property and human suffering caused by crowds getting out of control can be almost past belief. A *riot,* we might say, is the result of a number of people deciding to take the law into their own hands and then finding they don't know what to do with that decision.

QUESTIONS

1. Many writers have said in one way or another that the people in a mob adopt the thinking of the least intelligent member of the group and divide that intelligence among the others. What does such a statement mean?

   _____

   _____

2. Look up the legal meanings of "unlawful assembly" and "riot." Write those meanings in your own words.

   _____

   _____

3. Why do you suppose the laws set such a low number of people when they describe unlawful assembly or riot?

   _____

   _____

4. What exactly is a mob? _____

   _____

5. What causes riots to start? _____

   _____

   _____

6. Once started, how are riots stopped?

   _____

   _____

7. When mobs form and riots result, many laws get broken. What is the legal position of members of a mob? Are they all guilty of the crimes resulting from mob acts? Are rioters accessories to the crimes of the group? What defense could you give if you were arrested for taking part in a riot?

   _____

   _____

   _____

   _____

8. Looting usually goes along with riots. What is *looting?*

   _____

   _____

9. In cases of mob violence and riot, police and national guardsmen often arrest looters. At times, looters are roughed up or even shot. Why might law enforcement people be more likely to do physical violence to looters than to ordinary thieves?

   _____

   _____

14. Guilt by Association

There is no such crime as one called "guilt by association." *Guilt by association* is less a legal term than a social one. It means simply that if you are associated with a person or a group of people who get into trouble, you may be considered guilty even though you did not actually commit the crime.

Although the term "guilt by association" doesn't actually describe a certain crime, it is important because it can apply to so many legal situations. A person is assumed to be innocent until proven guilty. Many times police, juries, friends, and neighbors are willing to accept the idea of guilt by association as proof of actual guilt.

QUESTIONS

1. In your own words, tell what the term "guilt by association" means.

   _____

   _____

2. You and your friends are feeling good after leaving the movie theater. Several of you begin horsing around. One throws a rock at a passing car and breaks the windshield. Flying glass severely cuts the face of the little girl on the passenger side of the car. Based on the idea of guilt by association, how much trouble is each of you in?

   _____

   _____

3. Someone in your class steals the teacher's billfold from the bottom drawer of her desk. It's obvious that several students know who committed the theft. Are you all guilty by association? Why or why not?

   _____

   _____

4. You and a friend are in a department store. Your friend gets stopped at the door for shoplifting. Are you guilty by association?

_____

_____

5. When should people be punished because of their association with a person or persons who violated the law?

_____

_____

6. How can you defend yourself from the idea of guilt by association?

_____

_____

15. Accessory to a Crime

In a sense, the idea of being an *accessory* to a crime is pretty close to that of guilt by association. One is a legal term for a crime and the other is not. An *accessory* is a person who was perhaps not present at the time a crime was committed but who either knew that the crime was going to be committed or found out later and concealed knowledge or evidence of the crime.

An *accessory before the fact* is a person who knew in advance about the crime and even may have helped plan it. An *accessory after the fact* is one who helped conceal the crime after it happened or helped the person accused of the crime get away from the police. Both accessory charges are criminal violations of the law.

QUESTIONS

1. Why is the law so hard on people who are accessories, even though they did not actually help commit the crime?

_____

_____

2. Give two examples of cases in which a student your age might become involved as an accessory *before* the fact. These may be made-up examples or real ones, whichever you wish. Don't identify people in an actual situation.

_____

_____

Discuss the preceding examples in class.

3. Now describe two cases in which teenagers might become accessories *after* the fact. Give at least one example in which the involvement was by accident or without the person's knowledge.

_____

_____

Again, discuss these examples in class.

4. Why should the police and the courts either accept or not accept the excuse of accidental or unintentional involvement?

_____

_____

5. A young woman has been charged as an accessory to murder. It seems her friend shot and killed a fellow in a parking lot fight. The woman later drove her friend to another state. What defense can she give? What will the court most likely rule in her case?

_____

_____

6. How do the punishments for accessories to crime compare with those for persons who actually commit the crime?

_____

_____

16. Conspiracy

When we speak of the crime of conspiracy, we often have an idea of foreign spies sitting around, plotting to overthrow our government. Actually, anytime two or more people get together to plot or plan anything that is against the law, those people are guilty of the crime of *conspiracy*.

On first thought, this does not seem to be the sort of crime in which young people would be involved. On second thought, it is surprising that more young people don't end up being charged with conspiracy.

Think about the following situations. Discuss them in class and decide whether or not conspiracy exists.

(a) Four guys decide to beat up another guy who has been giving one of the four a bad time.

(b) A couple of fellows decide to hot-wire a car and drive around for a couple of hours.

(c) Three girls discuss how two of the group will distract the salesperson while the third shoplifts some items from the counter.

(d) A fifteen-year-old girl agrees to give an older friend money to buy a six-pack of beer, which the minor can't legally buy for herself.

(e) Several members of the class talk about creating a false fire alarm in order to miss a test.

QUESTIONS

1. Now that you have given some thought to conspiracy, think of times when you have been the possible victim of conspiracy. Remember that businesses can conspire against individuals.

   _____

   _____

2. When the whole group has had a chance to describe possible conspiracies of which they were victims, discuss the cases in class. Is each case discussed actually a conspiracy?

   _____

   _____

3. Are you more likely to be the victim of a conspiracy by people you know or by companies and corporations? Why?

   _____

   _____

17. Fraud

Fraud is just about anything that cheats another person out of rights or property. It covers a whole list of things from phony stock certificates to confidence games that take a person's life savings. A strange thing about the laws that deal with fraud is that so many things you and I might call fraud aren't called fraud by the law.

A good way to begin to understand fraud is to have one or more members of the class find out what your state laws say about fraud. Try to get a good definition. Also find out what the law says about proving that fraud exists.

QUESTIONS

---

1. Anyone who has anything to do with buying and selling things is likely to run into fraud. Think about some of your experiences. Can you think of four or five instances in which you were probably the victim of fraud? Describe them.

   _____

   _____

   _____

   _____

   _____

2. Now compare your answers with those of your classmates. Discuss the situations given. Try to decide whether the cases described were actually fraud. If they were not fraud, just what were they?

   Many things that look like fraud may be what a manufacturer, tradesperson, or other business-person calls "good business" practices or "just one of those things." A lot depends upon which side of the fence you are on.

3. As a group, decide whether the following situations might legally be called fraud.

   (a) A mechanic charges for changing an oil filter but doesn't, in fact, change the filter.

   (b) A shirt marked size sixteen shrinks two sizes when laundered.

   (c) You pay for a magazine subscription but receive no magazines.

   (d) The bank says it never received the deposit you mailed in.

   (e) Your boss says you worked only sixteen hours last week instead of the nineteen you know you put in.

   (f) The librarian says you did not return a book and charges you for it even though you remember handing it to her.

   (g) The supermarket advertises a "special" that is actually more expensive than the regular price.

   (h) The phone company makes an error and cuts off your phone service. When you show them the error, they charge you a fee to restore service.

4. As a consumer, what can you do to keep from becoming a victim of fraud?

   _____

   _____

18. School Laws

The role of the school depends upon two sets of rules. One set is made up of laws passed by the state legislature. The other set of rules is a set of policies passed by the board of education. Both the state laws and local school-board policies have a lot to do with your life during the dozen or so years you spend in school.

It is state school laws that determine how much education your teachers must have in order to teach. These same state laws decide how much schooling you must have.

Local school-board policies decide when school starts in the morning, what special programs will be offered, what school you will attend, and a thousand other things you probably never thought of.

Most school districts have a written set of policies concerning the school. It would be a good idea for your teacher to get a set of school policies for your class to use while studying this material.

QUESTIONS

1. What do the laws of your state say about attending school? What do your local school policies add to the state laws?

   _____

   _____

2. What penalties do either the laws or policies impose on students or their parents when attendance laws are broken?

   _____

   _____

3. Student conduct is a matter left up to the local schools. Without first checking on written policies, list the areas of student conduct you think your school covers in its policies.

   _____

   _____

   After the class compares and discusses the answers to this question on student conduct, check the written policies. See whether you missed some areas or noted some that are not covered by written rules.

   _____

   _____

4. Many schools have rules concerning students driving cars to school, leaving the school grounds for lunch, wearing certain types of clothing, and so on. Why should schools have the right to make rules dealing with such items?

_____

_____

5. Why might such rules be poor ones for schools and school boards to make?

_____

_____

6. What do your school policies say about book fees, library fines, shop charges, and other payments due to the school?

_____

_____

7. School districts have policies regarding suspension and expulsion of students. As a rule, suspension requires that a student remain home from school for anywhere from one to five days. In most cases the building principal can suspend a student. Expulsion means a student is prohibited from returning to school for a longer period of time, often for the remainder of the school year. Expulsion comes after a formal hearing and normally requires a vote of the school board.

   Under what conditions can the school tell you to stay home from school? What acts can result in suspension, and what activities call for expulsion?

_____

_____

8. Are there any school rules or policies that you believe are probably not legal and that may violate your personal rights? If so, which ones?

_____

_____

9. Are there school laws or policies that you feel should be made in order to make your school a better place in which to learn?

_____

10. Under what circumstances can students become involved with the courts for failure to obey school policies?

_____

_____

_____

19. Trespassing

It is pretty annoying when you want to go on a picnic and you find that everyplace you look is posted against trespassing. Signs saying "No Parking," "No Hunting," "No Trespassing" seem to cover the land. Whether it is in the country or in town, everywhere you turn there seem to be signs and warnings against using certain areas of land.

Even more annoying than trying to find a picnic spot is trying to find a place to park your car in a crowded city. Lot after lot of parking spaces flash by. Yet you can't enter them because they are reserved for employees or customers. Finally, in desperation you ignore a sign saying that parked cars will be towed away at the car owner's expense. You slip the car into an empty space and hurry to run your errands. When you return, you find that a wrecker has towed your car away.

QUESTIONS

1. Whether you live in the country or in the city, you are aware that many places are closed to trespassing. Describe some of these places and tell what the signs say.

_____

_____

2. Many public places, such as parks, playgrounds, and stadiums have signs on them indicating that the area is closed at certain times. Are there any such places where you live?

_____

_____

3. If there are, what do the signs say can happen if you violate the rule?

_____

_____

4. When dove-hunting season opened, Ted and Mike cleaned their shotguns and went hunting. The farmer's fields had no signs, so they crossed the fence. A few minutes later, the angry farmer arrived and told Ted and Mike he had called the sheriff and was charging them with criminal trespass. Will law enforcement officers get involved in something like this? Should they?

_____

_____

5. What defense can Ted and Mike give?

_____

6. Apartment complexes, private clubs, businesses, manufacturing sites, and residential areas often put up signs and even hire guards to prevent trespassing. What gives them the right to do this?

_____

_____

7. How far should a property owner be allowed to go in keeping trespassers from his property?

_____

_____

_____

8. What punishment or trouble can come your way from trespassing on another's land or property?

_____

_____

9. As people get more uptight about trespassing, what are some possible negative results?

_____

_____

_____

20. Pets Can Be Lawbreakers

Pets are an important part of many families. Most people care for their pets and provide them with proper living conditions. Very few pet owners give consideration to the legal side of pet ownership. When they do, it's usually because the police are at the door or a complaint and summons have just been handed to them.

QUESTIONS

1. First, let's consider the pet's point of view. What does the law say about improper care and mistreatment of pets?

_____

_____

2. Dog licenses are a yearly expense for dog owners. What is the penalty where you live for keeping an unlicensed dog? _____

_____

3. Are licenses required to keep other pets? If so, what pets, and what are the penalties for disobeying the law?

   _____

   _____

4. Leash laws are local ordinances that require dogs and perhaps other pets to be kept at home or on a leash. What are your local leash laws?

   _____

   _____

5. Does your city have a "clean streets" law for dogs? If so, how does it work?

   _____

   _____

6. What things can animals do that your city considers a nuisance? What penalties come from such animal behavior?

   _____

   _____

7. Does your city make any provision for keeping "exotic" pets such as lions and boas?

   _____

   _____

8. Are certain animals forbidden as pets by local ordinances? Why?

   _____

   _____

9. What is your legal responsibility if your dog bites someone who is on your property?

   _____

   _____

10. Assume your pet runs into the street and causes an accident when a driver tries to miss hitting him. Are you in legal trouble?

   _____

   _____

11. Does your city set limits on the number of pets you can own? If so, what does the law say?

   _____

   _____

12. Your adventurous pup takes off one evening with a bunch of his pals. The whole pack of dogs gets into trouble and ends up attacking farm animals or even a child. What does the law say about your dog and about you?

   _____

   _____

13. The dogcatcher (in many communities called an animal control officer) picks up your mutt for violation of the leash law or lack of a license. You have to pay to get your dog back or else the dog shelter will destroy it. Attack or defend this policy from the point of view of both the public and the animal owner.

   _____

   _____

   _____

   _____

14. There probably are more silly laws concerning animals than just about any other thing. In one city in the United States, for example, it is illegal to take a pig for a walk! Check the local ordinances for animal and pet laws. In addition to checking for answers to the preceding questions and others of your own, be on the lookout for really strange animal control ordinances.

21. Obscene Gestures, Filthy Talk, and Profanity

As a citizen of the United States, you are granted freedom of speech. So long as what you are saying is true and not intended to bring harm to another person, you are generally covered by this basic right. Of course, you discovered long ago that freedom of speech did not apply in certain circumstances, such as when the teacher was talking or when one of your parents was lecturing you about something you did that displeased them.

There are certain types of speech that are considered out of place and offensive by many people. Swearing and the use of vulgar or obscene terms are considered to be improper conduct by the majority in our nation. Making obscene gestures may be considered in the same light, since gestures are often taken to be an addition to speech.

It is very likely that you have heard a pretty good selection of obscene or filthy words and profanity. Obscene gestures probably aren't new, either. Whether or not these things offend you, and whether you have made use of them yourself, we won't ask.

QUESTIONS

1. We *will* ask you this: Why do people use these means of expression?

   _____

   _____

   _____

2. Since many people find these gestures and words offensive, shouldn't they have the right to be protected from seeing and hearing these actions and words?

   _____

   _____

3. Should freedom of speech cover the use of profane and obscene talk and gestures?

   _____

   _____

4. Some states have made it illegal to make an obscene gesture. Many states and cities have laws prohibiting public profanity. What do the laws in your state and town or city say about this?

   _____

   _____

   _____

5. As our society has changed, so have the feelings of many as to what may be said. Not all that many years ago, profanity and obscene words were never used in movies. Now they are quite common. Television now accepts mild swearing, and the daily newspaper no longer uses blanks or asterisks in place of such words in its direct quotes within news stories.

   Since the public has allowed the entertainment and news worlds to move in this direction, shouldn't you have the same rights in your own speech?

   _____

   _____

6. Should a school have the right to make rules against such speech and gestures even if the state laws do not make them illegal?

   _____

   _____

22. Libel, Slander, and Defamation

How many times have you heard someone saying things that were meant to hurt another person's reputation? How many times have *you* said mean or nasty things about someone else? Anger, hurt, and the desire to "get even" often cause people to say things about others that are better left unsaid.

The terms *libel, slander,* and *defamation* deal with writing and saying things about someone else that are intended to harm his or her reputation or to hold that person up to contempt. In defining each of these three terms, the word *malicious* is generally used. When you write or say malicious things to hurt another person's character, you may be guilty of one or more of the crimes of libel, slander, or defamation.

QUESTIONS

1. What does the word *malicious* mean?

   _____

   _____

2. Define each of the three legal terms:

   libel _____

   _____

   slander _____

   _____

   defamation _____

   _____

3. If you really "tell off" someone, are you guilty of one of these crimes? Why or why not?

   _____

   _____

   _____

4. Your boyfriend or girlfriend starts going with someone else. You write that person a long letter detailing all the faults your old flame has. Are you guilty of a crime?

   _____

   _____

5. You draw a picture or a cartoon that makes someone else out to be a fool. Have you committed a crime?

_____

_____

6. Newspapers carry political cartoons and editors write editorials. Some of these are quite blunt and even brutal. Why don't political cartoonists and newspaper editors get sued for such material?

_____

_____

7. If a person is charged with one or more of these crimes, there is one defense that can usually get the accused out of trouble. What is that defense?

_____

_____

8. Should there be limits as to what a person can write and say about another person even though what is written and said is true? Why or why not?

_____

_____

23. The Driver and the Law

Americans are more likely to be involved with the police and the courts over their automobiles than for any other single reason. This is because the automobile has become so much a part of our lives. As a result of the auto's extensive use, a great number of laws and ordinances have been passed to control its use. Constant use of the auto, coupled with the great number of rules, makes it highly likely that most of us will at some point break some of the rules either by accident or on purpose.

Since the laws dealing with autos are so frequently the cause of legal difficulties, we will spend some extra time on this area. Violations of automobile laws result in deaths, jail sentences, personal injury, property damage, lost time, and tremendous expense. For the average citizen, automobile laws offer the best chance to become a lawbreaker without even trying.

Every state and most cities pass special laws or ordinances covering motor vehicles. Generally, the basic state regulations may be obtained from the nearest driver license bureau. Some city police stations will provide copies of local statutes. Be sure to have copies of these driving rules in the classroom before beginning this section of *You and the Law.*

QUESTIONS

1. Without first looking at any written laws, list all the possible law violations you can think of that have to do with driving an automobile.

   _____

   _____

   _____

2. As a class, make a master list of everyone's ideas of possible auto violations.

3. The driver's license is a good place to start when learning about legal responsibilities. What different types of licenses are issued by your state?

   _____

   _____

4. Who is eligible for each type of license?

   _____

   _____

5. How can a driver lose the privilege to drive?

   _____

   _____

6. Do young or elderly people seem to have a greater chance of losing their licenses under your state laws? Why?

   _____

   _____

7. Many states have some sort of point system covering driving offenses. Various forms of improper driving gain points for the driver. A certain number of these penalty points acquired within a given time causes the driver to lose his or her license. If your state uses the point system, list those offenses that give a driver penalty points; note the number of points for each offense. If your state does not use a point system, describe the system in use.

   _____

   _____

   _____

   _____

8. Once you lose your driver's license, what may you do to regain the privilege to drive?

_____

_____

Improper use of the automobile can cause great personal injury and extensive property damage in seconds. For this reason, every driver should have liability insurance. This protects the innocent victims of a driver's mistakes. Collision and comprehensive insurance help pay for damage to one's auto.

9. Describe all the types of auto insurance with which you are familiar. Which are the more costly? Why?

_____

_____

_____

10. Are any forms of auto insurance required in your state in order to drive? If so, which ones?

_____

_____

11. What are the legal difficulties that can arise from driving without proper insurance?

_____

_____

12. What legal problems may result from causing an accident?

_____

_____

13. Now that you have considered some of the legal difficulties that can result from improper driving, give some thought to possible civil difficulties. What can you find out about the financial obligations of drivers who are involved in accidents?

_____

_____

_____

14. Careless and reckless driving are related, but legally they're worlds apart. What is the legal difference between these two offenses?

_____

_____

15. Drunk driving, or driving while impaired or what-ever your state calls the offense, is generally one of the most serious of all driving offenses. Not only does it cause a high percentage of fatal accidents, it also may result in extremely unpleasant legal action. How does your state define drunk driving and related charges?

_____

_____

16. What are the possible legal penalties for such offenses?

_____

_____

17. What is vehicular homicide, and what are the possible results of having this charge brought against you?

_____

_____

Earlier in *You and the Law*, we mentioned that an understanding of the law gives one freedom. We also said that ignorance of the law is never accepted in court as an excuse for breaking the law. Both these points apply equally in thinking about the law and driving. Know the law, obey the law, and drive as well as you possibly can. Even so, you will one day probably see a red or blue light in your mirror going blink, blink, blink. When that happens, try to remember that traffic rules were made to *protect* you, not to harass you.

24. Recreational Vehicles

The growing use of recreational vehicles by young people in America is an excellent indication of the country's affluence. This same affluence has brought about a body of laws. When only a small number of youths were involved with recreational vehicles, the need for legal control was slight. With growing numbers of youthful operators, the need for legal controls grew as well.

QUESTIONS

1. What is meant by a "recreational vehicle"? Name those that are common where you live.

_____

_____

_____

2. Public safety is an acceptable reason for the passage of a law. How does public safety fit into laws that deal with the use of recreational vehicles?

_____

_____

_____

3. Why should or shouldn't the law be able to control the use of recreational vehicles on private property?

_____

_____

_____

4. What do your local laws have to say in regard to young people who operate recreational vehicles?

_____

_____

_____

5. Drivers of motor vehicles are urged to carry liability insurance to protect others and their property in case of an accident. Do recreational vehicle operators have the same obligation? Should they?

_____

_____

_____

6. What would you suspect to be the more common legal difficulties people of your age get into concerning the ownership and operation of recreational vehicles?

_____

_____

_____

Review Quiz III

A. True or False

> **Directions:** Read each question carefully, and write either "T" (true) or "F" (false) in the space provided.

1. _____ Youths may be charged in juvenile court with guilt by association.

2. _____ A person not committing a crime may be charged as an accessory.

3. _____ When two or more people plan an unlawful act they are guilty of conspiracy.

4. _____ Your state may pass laws regarding the number of days students must attend school each year.

5. _____ Entering a home or piece of property without permission can result in a charge of trespass.

6. _____ Towns and cities may enact laws regarding punishment of owners of pets that are a nuisance.

7. _____ Profanity and obscene speech are protected under the Bill of Rights as freedom of speech in all situations.

8. _____ Slander may be termed defamation of character, but libel usually is not considered to defame another's character.

9. _____ Reckless driving is a more severe charge than careless driving.

10. _____ States and local communities establish driving laws and set penalties for breaking these laws.

B. Matching

> **Directions:** From the list at the right, choose the word or term that best matches each definition at the left. Write the letter of your choice in the space before the definition. Use each answer only once.

11. _____ Struggling with police officers

12. _____ A group of violently disorderly people

13. _____ A violent public disorder

14. _____ Robbing and plundering during a riot

15. _____ Having advance knowledge of a crime

16. _____ Learning of a previous crime and concealing knowledge of that crime

17. _____ Helping to plan a crime

18. _____ Cheating a person out of rights or property

19. _____ A policy-making body

20. _____ Unlawfully entering another's property

21. _____ Local rule regarding control of dogs

22. _____ Saying false things about a person

23. _____ Publishing untrue statements that damage another's reputation

24. _____ Marked by an intent to do harm

25. _____ Auto insurance that protects others from a driver's error

(a) looting

(b) conspiracy

(c) leash law

(d) libel

(e) resisting arrest

(f) fraud

(g) malicious

(h) mob

(i) liability

(j) accessory after the fact

(k) school board

(l) riot

(m) slander

(n) trespass

(o) accessory before the fact

25. Alcohol

Following the Second World War, the use of alcohol among teenagers was one of the nation's real problems. In recent years, it has again been recognized as a serious concern. Reports of twelve- and thirteen-year-old children who are alcoholics are not uncommon. In spite of laws dealing with the sale and use of alcoholic beverages, the problem of youthful drinking is further from being solved than it was thirty years ago.

QUESTIONS

1. Why do you think teenagers feel the need to drink alcohol?

   _____

   _____

2. Every state has its own laws concerning the purchase and use of alcoholic beverages. What does your state say about alcohol?

   _____

   _____

3. Find out what an "open container" law is and whether or not your city has such a law.

   _____

   _____

4. If a person who is under the legal drinking age manages to purchase an alcoholic beverage or have one bought for him, who is guilty of breaking the law, and how may such persons be punished?

   _____

   _____

5. Many parents allow their children to drink in their own home. Is this actually a violation of the law?

   _____

   _____

6. Shouldn't parents be allowed to bring up their own children as they see fit? Isn't learning to drink an important part of modern society?

   _____

   _____

7. How could our laws be changed to help solve the problem of teenage use of alcohol?

_____

_____

26. Drugs

The use of dangerous drugs, especially among teenagers, is a problem that involves the law, the home, and the community. The physical and mental problems attached to drug use are likely to be far more serious for many users than are the legal difficulties. Within recent years, many law enforcement officials and lawmakers have changed their views concerning drug laws. Prevention through education and rehabilitation rather than punishment is now quite often the goal of state and local laws and the law enforcement agencies.

QUESTIONS

1. Define what a dangerous drug is, name as many of them as you can, and describe their effects on users.

_____

_____

_____

_____

2. As a class, use the chalkboard to compile a master list of dangerous drugs from the individual lists made by students.

3. Marijuana may have appeared on some individual lists, but not on others. Why should or shouldn't it be on a list of dangerous drugs?

_____

_____

4. Do the laws of your state consider marijuana a dangerous drug?

_____

5. The laws in many areas distinguish between users and sellers of drugs. Also, the quantity of drugs found in a person's possession may have a lot to do with what charges are filed against that person arrested for drug violations. What do the laws where you live have to say about users and sellers, and the quantities of drugs in a person's possession?

_____

_____

_____

6. What provision is made for attempted rehabilitation of drug users?

_____

_____

7. At many gatherings (such as rock concerts), drugs are used openly. Police seldom make arrests in such cases. Why is such a policy good or bad?

_____

_____

8. You are at a party where drugs are being used, but you are not using them. Suddenly, you realize you are in the middle of a "drug bust." What is your legal situation?

_____

_____

9. Drug use and dependence often bring about other law violations. What law violations are often associated with drug usage?

_____

_____

10. Earlier in the text you learned that governments may seize or confiscate cars, boats, and homes used by drug dealers in their trade. You also learned that property believed to have been purchased with profits from drug dealing can also be taken by the government. How does this policy of property seizure affect people other than the drug dealers? Since law enforcement agencies are sometimes allowed to use some of the property and a portion of the money seized in drug raids, how may this affect law enforcement agencies?

_____

_____

_____

_____

11. In some places, laws have been proposed allowing the government to seize cars driven by those apprehended purchasing illegal drugs. How might such laws have both positive and negative results?

_____

_____

27. Sex Crimes

Not too many years ago, sex crimes were mostly associated with adult males attempting to lure young children into their cars. Once parents convince their children never to talk to strangers and never to accept rides or candy from strangers, it would seem that the problem of sex crimes would be solved.

This is not the case. The area of sex crimes is often quite involved, and it may result in extremely severe punishments for offenders. The laws in many states have changed regarding sex acts and sexually-related crimes. Certain acts once considered crimes in some states no longer result in prosecution. Homosexual activities between consenting adults are an example.

Even as laws regarding sex acts between adults have become more liberal, the penalties regarding sex crimes have tended to become more severe. This is especially true regarding sex crimes involving children as victims.

QUESTIONS

1. How would you define a sex crime? How many types of sex crimes involve youths of your age?

_____

_____

_____

_____

2. *Rape* is one of the most hated of all crimes. Many people have been sentenced to death for committing rape. What do the laws of your state say about rape?

_____

_____

_____

3. *Sex assault on a child* can be a special form of rape, which used to be known as statutory rape. It involves children under the age of legal consent. In general, this involves children sixteen years old and younger. However, a sex assault on a child does not have to involve force or the threat of it. For this reason it is a crime of special significance to youth.

    A charge of sex assault on a child may be filed against a young adult for having sexual relations with a younger, but willing, partner. The younger partner's parents may not go along with this, however. Charges may be filed, and the older partner is looking at major legal trouble. Or, a couple in which one member is legally an adult and the other several years younger may break up, and the younger member may file charges against the older partner for a sexual assault on a child.

    What makes the need for a law dealing with sex assault on a child necessary?

    _____

    _____

4. When may this law result in an unreasonable situation?

    _____

    _____

5. How young must a person be in your state in order to be the victim of sex assault on a child?

    _____

    _____

6. How does the punishment for sex assault on a child differ from that for rape?

    _____

    _____

7. Very closely related to the crime of rape are sex crimes that involve members of the same family or close relatives. *Incest* is the name given to the crime of engaging in sexual relations with a person too closely related for marriage. How does the law deal with incest?

    _____

    _____

8. *Homosexual acts* used to be classified as sex crimes in some states. This view is changing in many states in regard to homosexual adults. What does your state say regarding the actions of adult homosexuals?

    _____

    _____

9. Compare the punishments for sex crimes and the feelings about them with punishments and feelings for other crimes. Why is it that sex crimes are likely to be punished quite severely and cause such angry feelings among the members of the community?

_____

_____

10. In an effort to protect children, strict laws and severe punishments cover adults who involve children in *child pornography*.

    What is child pornography? If the child or children involved take part willingly, does this lessen the severity of the punishment for the adult or adults involved?

_____

_____

28. Abortion, Venereal Disease, and AIDS

We are considering abortion, venereal disease, and AIDS together for two reasons. They all result from having sexual relations. All three illustrate the fact our laws can and do change to keep pace with changes in the thinking of society. Recent laws generally have been far more liberal than was the case when your parents were your age.

Those people who support what is known as a right to life oppose abortion. They demonstrate in front of and near clinics that perform abortions. Additionally, they present legal challenges in the courts in an effort to repeal liberal laws dealing with a woman's right to an abortion.

Supreme Court rulings regarding abortion serve as legal guidelines for state laws. There seems to be little hope that those defending the right to abortion and those opposing it will ever agree, no matter how the nation's courts rule.

Abortion used to be legal only in rare cases, and then almost always only for married women. Usually the life of the expectant mother or her mental stability had to be threatened in order for a legal abortion to be performed.

QUESTIONS

1. What does your state say about abortion? Who may have an abortion? What reasons are legal justification for an abortion?

_____

_____

_____

2. Under what age must an unmarried woman have the consent of her parents for an abortion?

_____

3. Does a married woman have to have the consent of her husband? Should she?

_____

4. Must an unmarried woman reveal the name of the father? Should she?

_____

5. If an illegal abortion is performed, who has broken the law and what possible punishments may result?

_____

_____

Two cases concerning abortions received a lot of publicity. In one, a doctor was found guilty of homicide in the death of the fetus in an abortion. In the other, the doctor delivered a living fetus and deliberately allowed it to die.

6. Was the jury right or wrong when they found the first doctor guilty of killing a living being?

_____

_____

7. Was the second doctor legally correct when he allowed the living fetus to die?

_____

_____

8. In a number of areas of the nation, venereal disease among young people has become a serious health problem. Lots of people blame this on today's more liberal thought and attitudes. What could lawmakers, police, and judges do about the problem of venereal disease?

_____

_____

9. Many states allow teenagers to be treated for venereal disease without informing their parents. Why is this law good or bad?

_____

_____

10. What is the policy where you live?

_____

_____

11. In order to stop the spread of VD, doctors are required to report cases to local health departments. Is this a violation of a person's privacy?

    _____

    _____

12. Should a person with venereal disease who refuses to disclose names of sex partners be prosecuted? Why or why not?

    _____

    _____

13. The terror of AIDS became a worldwide problem in the 1980's. At first it was thought AIDS was primarily a problem of homosexual males. Soon doctors realized AIDS was capable of transmission among heterosexuals as well. By the 1990's, in some areas of the world AIDS spread faster among females than among males.

    In the United States, AIDS is to be feared equally by both sexes. Currently AIDS is an incurable disease, despite the fact that recent research holds promise of perhaps one day controlling the disease. AIDS remains the most fearsome health problem faced by the nation and the world in many years.

    The use of condoms is the best defense against acquiring AIDS sexually, other than having sex only with one AIDS-free partner or not having sex at all. Since this is the case, should schools and other social agencies distribute condoms and instructions for their use among the youths they serve?

    _____

    _____

14. Extremely conservative groups often oppose distribution of condoms and sexual information to minors. What do local laws and policies say regarding the rights of these groups as well as the rights of those who wish to make such distributions?

    _____

    _____

15. In Denver, a prostitute who tested positive for AIDS continued her trade despite court orders to cease selling sex. How should her situation be treated so that both her rights and the rights of those she might infect with AIDS are respected?

    _____

    _____

16. Those infected with the HIV virus can transmit it through unprotected sexual contact. HIV is, of course, the virus that causes AIDS. Some states have made it a crime to knowingly transmit HIV by having unprotected sex. Other states say knowingly transmitting HIV to another person is covered by existing laws regarding assault and attempted murder.

In 1996, a jury in Pueblo, Colorado, found a thirty-one-year-old rapist who sexually assaulted an eleven-year-old girl guilty of attempted murder. The judge sentenced the man to forty-eight years in prison.

Either support or oppose the jury's decision in this case as well as the judge's sentence.

_____

_____

_____

29. Disorderly Conduct, Disturbing the Peace, and Being a Public Nuisance

Many times people are enjoying themselves and having fun only to find their actions are disturbing other people. In such cases, people on both sides of the situation are likely to become unhappy. One person or group of people is unhappy at being disturbed. The other person or group is upset at being told to stop whatever activity is causing the disturbance.

These difficulties are by no means limited to teenagers. But young people quite often become involved in these problems either because they don't understand the situation or simply because they love life and enjoy living.

QUESTIONS

1. Define the three terms in the title of this section in your own words.

_____

_____

_____

2. What is the best way to keep from becoming involved in one or more of these charges?

_____

_____

3. Why are older people likely to be easily disturbed by the actions of teenagers? Don't they remember that they too were once young?

_____

_____

4. A number of cities have ordinances concerning noise disturbance. What things might such ordinances deal with? How might such disturbances be controlled?

_____

_____

5. A baseball game played under the lights has gone into extra innings. At 11:30 P.M., a neighbor calls the police. Are the fans and players violating the law?

   _____

   _____

6. Two guys get into an argument in a drive-in parking lot, and a crowd gathers to watch the fight. Has the law been broken? If so, who broke it?

   _____

   _____

7. Sexy Sammy walked down Main Street in a bikini that could be used as a bookmark. Heads turned and traffic stopped. Is Sammy guilty of one of the violations in the title? Why?

   _____

   _____

8. What might be disorderly or disturbing or a nuisance to one person might not be to another person nearby. This holds true even if the two people are the same age and the same sex. Who determines whether one of these violations has been committed?

   _____

   _____

9. If you and your friends found yourselves charged with one or more of these crimes, how might you go about preparing a defense to get you out of trouble?

   _____

   _____

30. Malicious Mischief and Vandalism

Exactly when does a prank become a case of *malicious mischief*? What pranks are just good jokes, and which ones are actually *malicious mischief* from the beginning? Every year, thousands of young people need to know the answers to these questions. In many instances, the answer comes while the youth and her parents face a juvenile officer or perhaps a juvenile court.

QUESTIONS

1. In your own words, tell what the term *malicious mischief* means to you.

   _____

   _____

   Have one class member check the legal meaning of this term.

   _____

   _____

2. Without giving the names of any participants, describe a case of malicious mischief you have heard about.

   _____

   _____

3. Have some volunteers read or describe some of these cases to the class. As a group, try to decide whether the instances given were actually malicious mischief or just jokes or pranks.

4. What is the official school-board policy in your school concerning cases of malicious mischief?

   _____

   _____

5. Newspapers often carry reports of *vandalism*. What does this term mean to you?

   _____

   _____

6. There have to be reasons for all actions. What are some possible reasons for people becoming involved in malicious mischief?

   _____

   _____

7. Why do you think people participate in acts of vandalism?

   _____

   _____

8. In your opinion, what part does the influence of a group play in some of these cases?

   _____

   _____

9. What would you suggest as reasonable ways that courts might handle cases of malicious mischief and vandalism?

_____

_____

31. Bomb Hoaxes

What better way is there to avoid an afternoon's classes than to phone in a bomb threat! Bomb threats are more disruptive than false fire alarms because it takes so much longer to check the building room by room for a hidden bomb than it does to locate a tripped fire alarm with no fire nearby. So long as the caller makes sure to disguise her voice and does not call from a private phone, she is safe enough. Or is she?

Phoning in a bomb threat is likely to cause the caller no end of difficulties when she is caught. Telephone companies, local courts, and school officials all take a dim view of bomb scares. The excuse "It was just a joke" seldom is sufficient to convince the authorities involved that the threat was a harmless prank.

QUESTIONS

1. What is the position of the telephone company regarding use of its equipment and services to notify a school or other public building of a supposed bomb?

_____

_____

2. What do your state and local statutes say about the seriousness of such a threat?

_____

_____

3. What policy does your local school board have concerning students who engage in such activities?

_____

_____

4. Now that you have explored the situation somewhat, let's look at some other angles that may be of interest to you before you decide to get out of a test by using a bomb hoax.

   You know that the telephone company takes a dim view of phoned bomb threats. What happens if you decide to mail your bomb threat? First of all, you must be careful to avoid leaving fingerprints on the letter or the envelope. You must be sure not to use a typewriter that can be traced, or even to write the threat in your own handwriting. Carefully printed block letters or letters and words cut from a newspaper seem to be your best bet.

(a) But before you sit down to compose your written hoax, what may happen to you as a result of using the United States mail to carry your threat?

_____

_____

(b) What federal laws are you breaking, and what federal agencies may become involved when you let the mail carrier do your dirty work for you?

_____

_____

5. By now, it should be fairly plain that a bomb hoax isn't the smartest way to get out of class on a warm spring afternoon. Here are a few problems to consider about bomb scares.

(a) Mrs. Reynolds rushes from her classroom when the intercom system alerts her to a possible bomb in the building. In her hurry, she leaves behind her purse containing her billfold and a fair amount of money. When Mrs. Reynolds returns to her room, her purse is not where she left it. When the bomb prankster is caught, what is his or her responsibility to Mrs. Reynolds?

_____

_____

Can the bomb prankster be named as an accessory to the theft?

_____

_____

(b) The teacher told Janice Hill and her classmates to get out of the room immediately. From the announcement that had come over the intercom, everyone realized it was a bomb threat. Recently Janice had read about a woman being blown to pieces when a bomb went off in a courthouse rest room. Frantic with fear, Janice started to run. In her fear and hurry, Janice did not see a pencil that had been dropped on the hall floor. When she stepped on the pencil, her ankle twisted and she felt the bone break with a sickening snap. What is the legal position of the bomb prankster in regard to Janice's injury?

_____

_____

32. Aggravated Assault

Anytime one person threatens another person with physical harm, that person has committed assault. When a person attacks another person with a dangerous weapon, the charge becomes *aggravated assault* and is more serious.

Fortunately, the law recognizes that some threats shouted in a moment of frustration aren't actually legal assaults. If this were not so, countless children would be in trouble from the often-heard threat, "I'll kill you for that!" Just when a threat becomes an assault may not be completely clear at times. When one person threatens or even attacks another with a weapon, however, it is quite clear that aggravated assault has taken place.

QUESTIONS

1. Without naming people or places, list some threats of physical violence you have heard made by or against friends recently.

   _____

   _____

2. In anger, teachers may tell students that they will break every bone in their bodies (or some other such statement) if they don't settle down. Are such statements assaults?

   _____

   _____

3. What if a student pulls out a switchblade and threatens to cut the teacher's throat?

   _____

   _____

4. How do the laws of your area deal with assault?

   _____

   _____

5. What do your laws say about aggravated assault?

   _____

   _____

6. You have probably run into the phrase *assault and battery*. *Assault* is the threat and *battery* is the actual striking or harming of another person. How would you say assault and battery differs from aggravated assault?

   _____

   _____

   _____

   _____

7. Would it be considered aggravated assault if a father whips his child with a leather belt? Explain your answer.

    _____

    _____

8. What if a school principal uses a board to paddle a student?

    _____

    _____

33. Concealed Weapons

In order to keep some crimes from happening, many states and cities have passed laws that prohibit people from carrying concealed weapons. The thinking behind such laws is easy to understand. People carrying concealed weapons are likely to be expecting or even looking for trouble. By not allowing anyone to carry concealed weapons, trouble can be avoided.

QUESTIONS

1. Under what circumstances should certain people be allowed to carry concealed weapons?

    _____

    _____

2. Concealed-weapons laws usually make clear what weapons they cover. However, the term weapon can be pretty broad. What are some things a young person might carry that might be considered concealed weapons?

    _____

    _____

3. Consider the case of the girl living in a neighborhood known for its high rate of street crime. Shouldn't she be allowed to carry some sort of weapon in her purse for her own protection?

    _____

    _____

4. Shouldn't an elderly woman in the same neighborhood be allowed to carry a protective weapon in her shopping basket?

    _____

    _____

5. Would your local police feel you were carrying a concealed weapon if you had a piece of pipe or other such item on the floor of your car?

   _____

   _____

6. In Colorado, it is still legal to wear a handgun so long as it is in open view and not worn in such a manner as to cause concern. (For instance, wearing a revolver into a bank is sure to cause problems.)

   Why should a person be allowed to do this when it is against the law to wear the same weapon beneath a coat?

   _____

   _____

   _____

7. The 1990's saw a move toward more liberal concealed-weapons laws in a number of states. Critics protested these laws, claiming this was an open invitation to more crime. It was their position that more people carrying concealed weapons would result in more gun-related crimes as these people used their weapons.

   Those who supported liberal concealed-weapons laws insisted that criminals are less likely to attack citizens when they know some of their intended victims may be armed.

   Interestingly enough, studies in Texas and Florida indicated that crimes against people dropped when more concealed-weapons permits were issued. In addition, the number of people with such permits who used their weapons to commit crimes was a tiny fraction of one percent of those licensed to carry concealed weapons.

   In 1996, a major University of Chicago study supported both previous studies and gave figures showing significant drops in crime rates in areas with liberal concealed-weapons laws.

   These studies indicate carrying concealed weapons may not be totally bad. Even with the drop in serious crime in such areas, there may be negative aspects of carrying concealed weapons. Defend this policy or oppose it. Refer to specific ideas concerning the law to support your position.

   _____

   _____

   _____

34. Murder, Manslaughter, and Homicide

Anytime one person takes the life of another, he or she is guilty of a *homicide*. There are several forms of homicide. Each form depends upon things such as the motive for the homicide and how the homicide was committed.

The crime of *murder* is the most serious of all homicides. It involves malice or the desire to do intentional harm. Charges of murder come from planned killings,  killings that occur during the time another crime is being committed, or killings for which there is no real excuse.

Manslaughter charges apply to killings that were not intended until the actual moment of the killing. Accidental killings often are called *negligent homicide.* Killings for which there is a legally recognized excuse are called *justifiable homicide* and have no legal penalties.

QUESTIONS

1. The juvenile codes in some states make it almost impossible for minors to be charged with the crime of murder. What do the laws where you live say about minors and murder?

   _____

   _____

2. What is the maximum penalty in your state for a person who is convicted of murder?

   _____

   _____

3. Have one student learn the differences between first- and second-degree murder and explain that difference to the rest of the class.

   _____

   _____

4. We can assume that you and your friends are not going to become involved in murder. There is one murder charge of which everyone should be aware, however. This is the charge of felony murder. A *felony murder* is a homicide in which a person dies as the result of a crime. In other words, a crime is committed and as a result, someone dies.

   Imagine two or three possible situations in which a person might be charged with a felony murder.

   _____

   _____

   _____

5. Compare these situations with those written by others in the class. For each case, decide whether the legal term of felony murder is justified.

6. There's a good possibility that a law-abiding citizen might be charged with negligent homicide. Such charges do not carry the death penalty. They are filed when a death is caused by some form of carelessness. By far the most likely situation is when a death results from an automobile

accident. Can you give another name by which negligent homicide is usually known when autos are involved?

_____

7. *Justifiable homicide* is the term used when soldiers or police officers kill another person in the legal course of their duties. Private citizens become involved in this situation when they take another person's life legally. Can you think of several cases in which a person might kill another and have it called justifiable homicide?

_____

_____

_____

8. *Manslaughter* is less serious than murder but far more serious than negligent homicide. This charge comes from killing another person without malice. It is most generally a spur-of-the-moment crime caused by passion. In your own words, tell what a "spur-of-the-moment crime caused by passion" means.

_____

_____

_____

9. Imagine several possible situations in which the charge of manslaughter rather than murder might be filed.

_____

_____

_____

_____

10. Have at least one member of the class find out whether a young person can be charged with manslaughter and what the possible penalty is for manslaughter. Another student can find out the difference between voluntary and involuntary manslaughter.

11. There is one crime in which a life is taken deliberately but for which the law can't punish the killer. What is it?

_____

12. People often argue that the *death penalty* (legal execution) is morally wrong. Their view is that deliberately taking a human life is a crime whether it is done by an individual or by a state. Others insist courts must be allowed to call for the death of some criminals in order to prevent others from committing certain crimes. What facts justify the death penalty? Which facts and moral questions indicate the death penalty should not be used?

_____

_____

_____

_____

35. Shoplifting

According to merchants, the crime of shoplifting raises the price of all goods. This is because merchants assume that a certain percentage of their goods will be shoplifted. The cost of that loss is added on to the cost of everything in the store so that the merchant can lose a certain amount of goods through shoplifting yet not lose any profit. When looked at in that light, shoplifting isn't a crime against the merchant but a crime against every consumer who buys from the merchant.

Shoplifting is generally thought of as a minor violation. Professional store thieves may rip off thousands of dollars in items from fashionable stores, but the average teenage shoplifter isn't in that league. Because of the generally rising crime rate, however, many police officers and judges have begun to view shoplifting as a major rather than a minor crime. In one example, a college student spent ten days in the county jail for shoplifting a ballpoint pen from a drugstore.

QUESTIONS

1. Exactly what is shoplifting?

_____

_____

2. Why do people shoplift?

_____

_____

3. Many stores hire store "detectives" to watch for shoplifters. These people apprehend shoplifters and hold them for the local police. What legal police powers do store "detectives" have? Can they force a suspect to answer questions? Can they legally detain a suspect for any length of time?

_____

_____

4. For a long time, most states ruled that a shoplifter could not be stopped unless he actually left the store with merchandise. In an effort to cut down on shoplifting, some states passed laws that allowed store owners to stop and hold suspected shoplifters who were still in the store. Why would this change in the law help control shoplifting?

_____

_____

5. What things seem totally wrong about such a law?

_____

_____

6. Shoplifting is a crime that comes under the heading of *larceny*. *Larceny* is broken up into two classes: *petty larceny* and *grand larceny*. Find out how your state defines both petty and grand larceny.

_____

_____

7. Which of the two violations are shoplifters most likely to be charged with and why?

_____

_____

8. Shoplifters or their parents usually offer to pay for the goods once they are caught. Why would a merchant be tempted to accept this offer?

_____

_____

9. Why would the police most likely want a merchant to prosecute rather than accept payment?

_____

_____

36. Larceny, Robbery, and Burglary

The three words in the title all add up to the same things—taking something that isn't yours. Stealing and theft are two more commonly used words that have similar meanings. Although all three terms are alike in that they have to do with theft, they are quite different in the eyes of the law.

Larceny is a fancy word for any kind of stealing. *Robbery* means force, or the threat of force, was used. *Burglary* has to do with breaking and entering, or going into someone else's home or buildings with the intent to commit a crime.

QUESTIONS

1. As you have previously learned, the crime of larceny is divided into two categories. *Petty larceny* is stealing an item of small value, and *grand larceny* covers the theft of more valuable items. In your state, at what point does petty larceny become grand larceny?

   _____

2. How does the punishment for grand larceny differ from that for petty larceny?

   _____

   _____

3. Robbery is quite often called *armed robbery*. The reason is quite simple. Since robbery means force was used or threatened, armed robbery is probably the most common sort of robbery. How much trouble is an armed robber in compared to an ordinary shoplifter or thief?

   _____

   _____

   _____

4. *Burglary* used to mean entering another person's house or building at night. Now it can take place at any time in many if not most states. The interesting thing about the crime of burglary is that you can be in trouble even if you don't steal anything. Just the fact that you entered someone's home or business with the *intent* to commit a crime is enough to get you charged with burglary.

   Before going any further, tell exactly what things cause youths your age to get involved in larceny, robbery, and burglary.

   _____

   _____

   _____

   _____

5. If one person takes another's bike, what is the crime? Why?

   _____

   _____

6. A couple of tough-looking guys suggest that if you don't hand over your money, you will need a good health insurance policy. What are they guilty of? Why?

   _____

   _____

7. You "forgot" to pay for a pen-and-pencil set. Which of the three crimes have you committed, and why?

_____

_____

8. The garage filled with antique furniture was just too much of a temptation. The owner caught the youth just after the boy had pried the lock from the door. Will the boy be charged with burglary? Explain your answer.

_____

_____

37. Possession of Stolen Property

Receiving or possessing stolen property is a sure way of getting into bad trouble. We have already mentioned this as a crime that may not seem all that serious. In fact, it may bring a tougher charge than actually stealing.

QUESTIONS

1. Why do you suppose laws deal so harshly with those who have stolen property in their possession even though they did not steal it?

_____

_____

2. Possession of stolen property might in some cases be called an "accidental" crime. How might it be called that?

_____

_____

3. A friend offered to sell you his ten-speed for a good price. You accepted and paid for it. A month later, you were picked up by a police officer because you were riding the ten-speed that had been stolen six weeks before. What sort of trouble are you in?

_____

_____

4. Your friend has already spent the money you paid him for the bike. He says he bought it from a guy he didn't know. The police say he stole it. Who gets the bike?

_____

_____

5. How do you get your money back if you aren't the one who gets the bike?

_____

_____

6. How can you be sure you are safe from ever getting involved with receiving or possessing stolen property?

_____

_____

38. Computer Crime

Computer crime is one product of a constantly changing society. This form of criminal activity has come into being in recent years only because computers now play such an important part in our daily lives.

In order to have computer crime, we not only need to have computers but also need the mastery of computers and their operation necessary to commit crimes with them.

QUESTIONS

1. Computer crime is often referred to as an offense committed largely by young people. Why would this statement be made, and is it valid?

_____

_____

2. When does hacking stop being innocent fun as the result of curiosity and become criminal activity?

_____

_____

3. Many teenagers use computer bulletin boards that share information, computer data, and software. Under what circumstances might bulletin board users become involved in illegal activities, often without ever intending to break the law?

_____

_____

4. The term *computer virus* came into being in the 1980's. This term promises to be a part of our vocabulary from now on. As you well know, a "virus" is devised by one who is skilled in computer programming. The virus spreads to or infects networked computers or computers that share infected software. The virus may be relatively harmless and do simple things such as display a

comic message when certain computer processes occur. It may be extremely harmful and begin to destroy data or cause a computer or computer system to crash.

Of what are computer programmers guilty when they devise a virus and cause that virus to spread to the computers of innocent users? What sort of punishment is justified in such cases?

_____

_____

5. Consider each of the following three cases. Decide whether a crime was committed in each case and what sort of punishment is likely when the computer programmer is caught.

   (a) Sara knew more about computers than anyone in her school, including the computer instructor. For this reason she was assigned to enter material into the school computer as part of her leadership assignment. It would be fun, Sara thought, to give a few of her friends better grades than their teachers did.

_____

   (b) When Linda was told she was going to lose her job, it made her furious. On her last day at work, she entered a number of destructive commands into the company's computer. The following day, sales information suddenly vanished, employee records were altered, and income tax figures were scrambled.

_____

   (c) William had worked at the First City Bank for over two years and understood all there was to know about its account records. Just as an experiment, he programmed commands into the bank's computer that automatically began adding small deposits to the accounts of customers William picked at random. When his handiwork went undetected, William decided it was time to broaden his outlook. He entered a program that ordered the computer to make deposits to William's account and to the accounts of his family members at various times for odd amounts.

_____

_____

6. Although business and industry were reluctant to bring charges against computer criminals for a number of years, the trend now seems to be toward sending computer criminals to prison. What is the difference between a hacker and a criminal?

_____

_____

7. Computer software can be extremely expensive. It is common for computer users to share software. One user buys a program and makes copies to share with friends. In the case of free shareware downloaded from a network, this is generally legal. Copying and distribution of commercial programs purchased from a store or from a network is a violation of copyright law. The producer of the software is entitled to a royalty from each copy used.

Obviously, companies and nations that violate computer software copyright are committing crimes. But what about the individual user who makes copies for just a few friends (who in turn make copies for their friends)? Should individuals be prosecuted for violating copyright law? If so, what is a reasonable punishment? If not, why not?

_____

_____

_____

39. The Working Student

There are a number of laws that apply to you when you are working for another person or company. Many of these laws are taken for granted. Others are never known or at least not understood by young employees. The laws dealing with employees are of great importance, though. Some affect workers daily, while others apply only after certain things have happened.

Let's think about some of the laws that apply to you as a working student.

QUESTIONS

1. Certain minimum working ages are set by law. Why were such laws passed?

_____

_____

2. Under what circumstances may such laws be harmful?

_____

_____

3. The federal government has set certain minimum wages that must be paid to workers. Do they cover all the jobs at which teenagers work?

_____

_____

4. Other than for odd jobs such as lawn work, no worker can be hired without having a Social Security number. What is Social Security, and what does it do for you?

_____

_____

5. The federal government and most state governments require the employer to take income taxes from the earnings of all workers. How do these income tax laws affect you when you work part-time or during vacations?

_____

_____

6. States have laws that require employers to carry workmen's compensation insurance on their workers. Are minors covered by such insurance policies? If so, how does such insurance work?

_____

_____

7. If an employer fires a teenage worker for no good reason, does the worker have any protection under the law? Should he?

_____

_____

8. Can an out-of-work teenager receive unemployment benefits?

_____

_____

9. If a youthful worker follows his employer's instructions and gets into trouble as a result, what sort of problems does the worker have legally?

_____

_____

10. What can a young employee do if his employer refuses to pay him or pays less than promised?

_____

_____

40. Youth as Consumers

Laws protecting consumers have been terribly slow in coming. Those consumer protection laws now in force often are not able to do an adequate job of actually protecting the consumer. New consumer protection laws are sometimes proposed, but few seem to become law. Those that do often are changed within a few years to less effective measures.

It seems reasonable to predict that more attention will be given to laws guarding the rights of consumers. Most of these laws probably will not come quickly. When they do become law, many consumers will still feel the need for more and better consumer protection laws.

Since consumer laws and consumer protection cover enough material for an entire book, we'll only touch on a few areas here.

QUESTIONS

1. When a consumer borrows money or uses credit, he or she is covered by the *Truth in Lending* law. What is the purpose of this law? How does it protect the consumer? When does it come into use?

_____

_____

2. If you, as a minor, wish to borrow money or use credit, how do you go about it? Are you protected in any way? Is the merchant with whom you deal protected?

_____

_____

3. Minors are constantly buying items from merchants. In many instances, some adjustment is necessary. Perhaps clothing does not fit, or an item does not work correctly. Do minors have the same rights as an adult when it comes to exchanging or getting refunds from merchants?

_____

_____

4. Many young drivers pay for their own cars and then pay for the expenses of running them. Such expenses include repair work. There probably is no area of consumer protection, or lack of protection, that has received more publicity than auto repairs. Claims of overcharging, sloppy work, or undone work are common in this area. What things should a youthful driver be aware of before taking her car to a garage for repair?

_____

_____

_____

5. Students are forever joining book clubs, record clubs, model clubs, and other groups that require the member to make a monthly purchase. If a student refuses to pay for the items he or she has received, what can the organization do about it?

_____

_____

6. If the organization sends things the member does not want or demands payment for things the student never received, does the student have any protection at all?

_____

_____

7. Another thing students do quite often is order merchandise from magazine advertisers. What basic precautions should you always take when ordering things by mail?

_____

_____

8. The United States Postal Service operates a system for investigating mail fraud. Have one or two members of your class meet with the local mail inspector to learn what the Post Office can and will do to help the consumer in cases involving nondelivery of items advertised through the mails. These students should take with them a list of questions prepared by the class before the interview. After meeting with the mail inspector, the students should report back to the class. Most of you will probably be upset when you learn exactly what the Post Office will and won't do to protect you.

9. Lots of students have their own credit cards or are allowed to use their parents' credit cards and charge accounts. Others can write checks on either their own or their parents' accounts. What is necessary for minors to be able to use credit cards and checking accounts?

_____

_____

10. If a minor charges items his parents can't afford or writes worthless checks, what can happen as a result?

_____

_____

11. When a person contracts to buy or sell something, the contract becomes legally enforceable. This means that if one of the parties who made the contract does not live up to the contract, the other party can take him to court. In most states, minors have quite a bit of protection when it comes to making and breaking contracts. Find out how contracts made by minors are treated where you live. Decide whether the protections given minors are good or bad, and why.

_____

_____

41. When the Law Picks on You

Nobody likes to be picked on. Many people hate to acknowledge that the law picks on some people. Young people can get picked on by the law, perhaps without even knowing it. Let's finish things by finding some examples of how you can be a victim of the law.

QUESTIONS

1. You have just pulled a really stupid trick. It is one of those things you don't want anyone to know about. The police insist upon calling your parents, however, and the juvenile court insists that your parents attend your hearing. If you were an adult, they wouldn't do this. Why do they now? Have any of your rights been violated?

   _____

   _____

2. You have just gotten your first traffic ticket. The officer mentions that if you are found guilty, it will mean the loss of your license. Adults in your state can have several such tickets without losing their right to drive. Why are young drivers picked on?

   _____

   _____

3. If six or eight of the guys happen to get together and are standing on a street corner talking, a police officer is likely to tell them to "break it up," or something. If six or eight businessmen happened to meet on the same corner, the cop probably would ignore them or smile and wave. Why does he pick on you, and why does the law allow it?

   _____

   _____

   _____

4. You have saved your money to buy a car. When the time comes to buy it, you find that the laws of your state require the title to be put in an adult's name. It's your money, but the law says it isn't really your car. Is this fair?

   _____

   _____

5. You and your girlfriend are in love and have decided to get married. The law in your state says neither of you can marry without the consent of your parents. You are old enough to pay taxes, but you still have to get permission to marry. Why does the law pick on you like this?

    _____

    _____

6. There's a movie you want to see, but it's rated "R." The cashier shakes her head and tells you that you aren't old enough to go in without your parents. Yet you have been paying adult prices since you were twelve. Why does the law let the motion picture theaters pick on you?

    _____

    _____

7. For two years you have worked part-time and also during the summer. This summer you can't find a job, no matter how hard you look. When you try to apply for unemployment benefits, you are told you don't qualify. Yet when you were working after school, on weekends, and during vacation, the government was always happy to take income taxes and Social Security payments out of your paycheck. What's going on?

    _____

    _____

8. Now that you have given some thought to these areas, look around you and find some situations in which the law either picks on you or allows others to pick on you. Write them up and then discuss them with the class.

    _____

    _____

We said earlier that the law isn't perfect. The only way it can come even close to perfection is for everyone to understand what it should do and then work toward that end. When the law picks on you, it may be for a reason you don't see at first, or it may be simply because nobody in the lawmaking business ever looked at it from your point of view.

Review Quiz IV

A. True or False

> **Directions:** Read each question carefully, and write either "T" (true) or "F" (false) in the space provided.

1. _____ Marijuana and crack are considered the same in the eyes of the law.

2. _____ An act that offends public morals may be considered disorderly conduct.

3. _____ Vandalism involves deliberately harming or destroying property.

4. _____ Aggravated assault charges may be filed when a person threatens to harm someone who has aggravated him or her.

5. _____ Only knives, guns, or blackjacks are concealed weapons.

6. _____ Anytime one person takes the life of another, a homicide has occurred.

7. _____ An accidental killing may be termed negligent homicide.

8. _____ A vehicular homicide may be a negligent homicide.

9. _____ Any kind of theft is larceny.

10. _____ Taking another's property through force or threat of force is robbery.

11. _____ Computer hacking by a minor cannot result in legal difficulties.

12. _____ Young traffic offenders may lose their driving licenses for offenses that would not take the license from an adult driver.

13. _____ States may prohibit youths from holding certain jobs.

14. _____ A crime-of-passion killing may result in a charge of manslaughter.

15. _____ More youths are charged with murder than with larceny or assault.

B. Sentence Completions

> **Directions:** Underline the word or term in parentheses that makes each statement correct.

16. One way communities fight public drunkenness is with (*open container, legal hour*) laws.

17. An adult can be charged with sex (*assault, attack*) on a child even if the young person willingly engaged in sex with the adult.

18. One type of killing that the law does not punish is (*homicide, suicide*).

19. A person who fills his or her yard with discarded appliances and junk autos could be charged with (*being a public nuisance, disturbing the peace, disorderly conduct*).

20. Using the mails to deliver a bomb threat is a (*state, local, federal crime*).

21. Threatening to harm another person may result in a charge of (*battery, assault*).

22. The most serious of all killings is (*homicide, manslaughter, murder*).

23. A death that is the result of another crime is (*manslaughter, felony murder, negligent homicide*).

24. Shoplifting is likely to be considered (*petty, grand*) larceny.

25. Entering the home or property of another with the intent to commit a crime may be considered (*larceny, robbery, burglary*).

Part III

You, Your Family, the Law, and Current News

Introduction

The law is in the news on a daily basis. If you look beyond the basic reporting of crime, there is a multitude of legal news in the daily newspaper and on nearly every television newscast. The legal point in the day's news may have to do with something the legislature is considering on a state or federal level. It may be concerned with a change in zoning the town council is weighing or a policy the local school board is studying.

Our laws are not static. Laws grow and change just as students do. Children become youths who grow into adulthood. Laws grow and mature in an attempt to meet the needs of a changing society. Some legal problems are as old as human history. Our legal system continues attempts to provide workable solutions to such intractable problems. Other problems facing our legal system are the result of changes in our society. Fifty years ago there was no need to consider laws to govern the World Wide Web or computers linked to the Internet. Today these areas are of major concern.

As our legal system attempts to provide for the needs of not only today's population but also those yet to be born, new laws are made and existing laws are modified. No matter how hard our lawmakers try to keep up, they seem always short of complete success. Quite often it becomes a case of passing a law after it is too late to prevent a crime and protect the innocent or passing laws that seem unfair to portions of our population.

Even when laws are passed, there is no guarantee they will do what citizens and lawmakers intended. This is due, in part, to the human mind. Intelligent criminals and resourceful lawyers are often capable of circumventing even the best-intentioned laws.

And then there is the process of judicial interpretation. A judge or a number of judges may study a newly enacted law and see complications or ramifications the lawmakers overlooked or never dreamed possible. In this way a law intended to provide for certain protections and punishments may be ruled unconstitutional by the court system. Or it may be interpreted in an entirely different manner than lawmakers anticipated.

Not all laws are good. Most are intended to serve the community, the state, or the nation. A few laws get passed that are poorly thought out. These we attempt to change when it becomes obvious they aren't working.

Despite the fact that we live in a time during which laws are passed left and right, we are all aware of the fact that it is really respect for the principles of law that enables us to function as a society. Willingness to obey, or attempt to obey, the law allows us to live together in relative harmony. Passing a law does not guarantee a change in behavior or protection of the innocent. When a law is enacted, it serves as a guideline for living. The rest is up to those covered by the law. In this section of *You and the Law,* we'll cover some legal items right out of the current news. Though some appear not to affect you directly, all have a bearing on you and your family simply because you live in our nation.

Consider these current legal problems. Then, as you watch the news or read the daily paper, be aware of the constant efforts of our laws to keep pace with the needs of our society.

42. Curfews for Children and Youths

The idea of curfews is not new. Curfews date back in history to the time the gates in the town walls closed at night to protect the local citizens from attack by outsiders. A person returning to town late was forced to spend the night outside the protection of the city walls.

Curfews are intended to keep people off the streets at night and in the safety of their homes. Many centuries ago the curfew helped night watchmen identify potential criminals. Anyone out on the streets after curfew was likely up to no good and subject to arrest.

Today's curfew laws work in much the same way as did those years ago. They are a city's attempt to keep children and youths below given ages out of trouble. Statistically, cities can show that when children and youths are unsupervised on the streets during certain hours, they are more likely to be involved in crimes than at other hours. This does not mean just that children and youths commit more crimes at 2:00 A.M. than at 2:00 P.M. It also means they are more likely to be the *victims* of crimes during the late night hours than at other times of the day. Those who support the idea of curfews for children and youths argue that they are trying to protect those covered by the curfew from crime as much as they are attempting to protect innocent victims from youthful criminal activity.

Curfews set a time after which it is a violation of local law for children and youths to be out of their homes. Generally a time such as 11:00 P.M. for weeknights and perhaps midnight or 1:00 A.M. on weekends is set as the curfew. Students accompanied by their parents are not covered by curfews. Students who are taking part in an organized school activity, such as returning from an out-of-town ball game or a concert, are not bound by the curfew hours. The idea of the curfew is to cut down on the number of unsupervised children and youths roaming the city streets late at night.

In some cities those picked up by the police for curfew violation are taken home. In other places curfew violators are taken to a holding center, such as a school gym or similar location. Their parents are called and required to come to pick up their sons or daughters.

Often some form of counseling is given to those brought into these centers. Parents must sometimes talk with counselors. Depending upon the city, curfew breakers and their parents may be required to appear before a juvenile judge for a hearing after violating the law a certain number of times.

Some children and youths view curfews as a violation of their civil rights. Many parents feel the same way. Other parents and their children accept the idea of a curfew as a means of protecting children from crime and from becoming involved in criminal acts.

Whether the curfew idea is successful is open to question. What is without question is that having a curfew is one way in which the law is attempting to meet the needs of today's society.

QUESTIONS

1. Consider the idea that a curfew violates the civil rights of students your age. In what way may it violate your rights?

_____

_____

2. Critics of curfews protest that teenagers who work late may become victims of curfew times when returning home from work. Those supporting curfews counter by saying teenagers should not be working this late at night. Which side of this argument is more valid, and why?

_____

_____

3. What are some obvious things that can go wrong with curfew laws? Consider cost of the program, parental actions, and the court system for starters.

_____

_____

43. Graffiti and Tagging— Both Are Vandalism

By 1995 the police and citizens of New York City made a discovery. The policy of cracking down on those engaged in minor criminal activity such as spraying graffiti paid off in an amazing manner. New police policies called for arrest of graffiti sprayers as well as for other vandals. To the surprise of many, the overall crime rate in New York City declined.

To those responsible for the stricter enforcement of New York City's laws, the decrease in crime rate came as no surprise. These citizens maintained that writing graffiti and similar crimes, when left unpunished, encouraged more serious crime. Offenders might think that if not punished for vandalism, they wouldn't be punished for theft, arson, rape, or even murder.

Law enforcement representatives came to New York City from across the nation and around the world to see how the new policies worked. Many people did not see the relationship between allowing one sort of crime to go unpunished and the growth of other crimes.

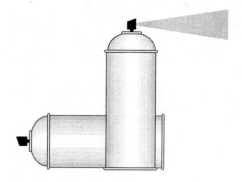

Graffiti has long been associated with gangs staking out territory. Some people have excused graffiti as a means of youth expressing themselves and seeking identity. Many have felt that graffiti was bad but that artistic tagging was all right. Taggers created interesting and often beautiful artworks. To the owner of the spray-painted building, graffiti and tagging are one and the same. Both are forms of vandalism.

Most law enforcement officials now realize that if graffiti is allowed to remain and spread, it encourages other forms of antisocial activity, not the least of which is growth of gang influence. Experience also indicates that quick removal of graffiti tends to discourage vandals from repeating their acts. City councils have enacted ordinances requiring the removal of graffiti. In many locations the property owner is legally required to paint over or otherwise remove graffiti and tagging within a certain length of time. Otherwise the city will have it removed and bill the property owner. In some places groups of volunteers go out weekly or monthly to scrub off and paint over graffiti in public and even private locations. A few cities and towns now require apprehended graffiti sprayers and taggers to remove their work and the work of others as part of their punishment.

In an effort to end this form of vandalism, some cities and states have enacted laws making it a crime for a merchant to sell spray paint to minors. There are so many ways for graffiti sprayers and taggers to get around these laws that it is doubtful they have a major effect on the problem of graffiti. However, like so many efforts, such laws are an attempt to find a solution to a problem.

No matter where it appears or why it is done, the spraying of graffiti is likely to be considered vandalism. (Consider this: In ancient Rome graffiti brought the death penalty.)

QUESTIONS

1. Requiring the owner of private property to bear the cost of removing graffiti punishes an innocent party for another's criminal act. Is there a better way of dealing with the problem? Or, is the greater good accomplished by removal of the graffiti justification for the cost to an innocent individual?

_____

_____

2. When volunteers donate time and effort to remove graffiti, they help stop its spread. What else is accomplished as a result of the efforts of volunteers?

_____

_____

3. Is tagging the same as gang- or other identity-related graffiti? Should taggers be treated the same as graffiti vandals?

_____

_____

44. Bombs Create Such Great Effects

There it is. Right in front of you. Fresh off the Internet. In words and diagram are directions for building a great explosive device. Let's not call it a bomb. Let's call it a noisemaker.

All that is required is a plastic bottle and some stuff that's easy to get. Then, within a minute, you can turn the bottle into a device that will blow the sides out of a mailbox, destroy a trash can, and scare the living daylights out of everyone within fifty yards of the explosion. What a trip!

"But dig this. Check out this book I just bought. Here are instructions for making a pipe bomb that makes the plastic bottle device look like child's play. It even tells where we can buy black powder just like the people who fire old-fashioned muzzle-loading rifles they build from kits."

"Look at the chapter in this book I checked out from the library. It tells how to make all sorts of explosive devices."

In August 1996, a seventy-five-year-old man in the authors' home state suffered burns and other injuries when a root beer bottle filled with chemicals exploded when he opened his mailbox. Law officers did not feel the elderly man was a deliberate target. They suspected the bottle bomb was intended to blow up the mailbox. The unfortunate man opened it at just the time the chemicals had done their thing and were ready to explode.

The previous year a young child found a pipe bomb and lost part of his hand when it blew up as he played with it.

When a noisemaking explosive device goes off in the wrong place at the wrong time, its makers are instantly guilty of a felony. In today's world anyone making or transporting an explosive device is most likely to be treated as a criminal.

QUESTIONS

1. Instructions for making bottle bombs, pipe bombs, and other similar devices can be found on the Internet, at the magazine stand, and even in the public library. If a person makes use of these directions, is he or she totally at fault if the device causes injury or damage?

   _____

   _____

   _____

2. Federal laws prohibit making explosive devices. What if you own a large area of land well away from neighbors and the closest town? Why shouldn't you be allowed to make and explode plastic bottle bombs on your own property? Don't you have the right to do something that does not harm others?

   _____

   _____

3. Several engineering students exploded a plastic bottle "noisemaker" in their college dorm and destroyed several ceiling panels. It was just a more successful prank than they realized it might be. Police were called. What would be a reasonable punishment in this instance? What might be the most severe punishments these students could receive?

_____

_____

45. Moving Targets Add to the Fun

Years ago paint ballers began spending weekends "hunting" one another through the woods and in special survival courses. The object was, of course, to shoot your opponents with a special gun that fired a paint ball before one of them shot you with his paint ball.

Then came the laser guns, which fired beams of light and registered "hits" as they were made. Old warehouses were turned into hunting grounds for laser gunners.

Blowguns and small metal darts for target practice made the scene in some locations. These were a major step up from the old plastic bean shooters popular a generation or two ago.

The laser gun craze didn't last long but did survive long enough for children playing with them in a school yard to come close to losing their lives. Neighbors saw the light flashes in the dark and assumed real weapons were being fired. (No, the laser guns did not make the sound of a weapon. The neighbors were spooked due to previous weapon use in the area.) When police arrived, officers saw the flashes and thought they were being fired on. No one was killed, fortunately.

National television audiences viewed scenes videotaped by youths as they drove through city streets firing paint-ball guns at pedestrians, bicyclists, and other motorists. The youths were captured, arrested, and charged with a multitude of felonies.

In a small city several high school-age students had a grand time firing small metal darts into the bodies of passersby. They used a silent, easily hidden blowgun.

Instances of backyard archery going wrong are all too common. Accidentally or on purpose, neighborhood animals and children become victims of arrows, causing serious injury and even death.

The legal consequences of misuse of pseudo-weapons, bows and arrows, compressed air guns, and the like, can be major.

QUESTIONS

1. In the case of the laser guns, should the police officers have been charged had one of them shot a child who pointed the laser gun at the officers?

_____

_____

2. Paint-ball guns are intended to be fired at human beings. Unless the victim is wearing a heavy shirt and trousers, the paint ball's impact is painful but not serious. Goggles avoid eye injuries. In the case of the car of youths firing at those they passed, of what crimes were they guilty?

_____

_____

_____

3. Those involved in the videotaped paint-ball incident did not intend to kill anyone. They probably didn't really want to hurt anyone. What is their best defense?

_____

_____

4. What is the legal liability for the archer whose arrow leaves the yard and injures a neighbor? What is the archer's civil liability? What defense can the archer offer?

_____

_____

_____

46. It Was Just a Prank— We Were Only Having Fun

A prank is just a harmless joke. It's just another way of having fun. The question is, at what point does a prank turn into a major legal problem?

Most pranks begin as a result of youthful good spirits. Sometimes boredom causes pranks to be born. At times a desire to get even or extract revenge may result in a prank.

Whatever the cause, an April Fool's-type joke is one thing. A prank that causes harm to property, fear to individuals, or physical injury is no longer a prank. At this point it is a crime.

There are those among us who can't resist the urge to fill balloons with water on beautiful days and lob them at a friend. When the target of water balloons becomes pedestrians walking along the street or passing below an apartment window, the joke is over. Not only do the exploding balloons frighten unsuspecting victims, a water balloon dropped from even a moderate height can cause serious injury. Tossing water balloons from a speeding car has been a sport for some of us over the decades. A water balloon crashing into a windshield, entering an open driver-side window, or hitting a pedestrian in the face is almost certain to cause injury.

How about the time-honored trick of gathering real estate signs from lawns and placing them on the lawn of a friend, an enemy, or a school principal?

A variation of the real estate sign prank came when a group of teenagers in an upscale neighborhood decided it would be great fun to remove all the Neighborhood Watch signs from the area. How better to let the home owners know they weren't really watching all that care-fully? The problem came when officials noted the cost of each Neighborhood Watch sign in the area was $20. About fifty were stolen. In that state any theft of more than $400 is prosecuted as a felony. Since all fifty signs were taken in one sweep of the neighborhood, the multiple thefts were classed as one grand theft. Suddenly a "harmless" prank meant possible big-time trouble.

And then there is the sport known as mail-box bashing. The passenger in a car has a base-ball bat in hand. Each time the car nears a mailbox, the driver swerves toward the mailbox,

and the baseball bat is used to smash it. Unhappy home owners can either attempt to bend the ruined mailbox back into shape or buy a new one. As for the person whose mail was still in the box but is now scattered to the winds, it just added to the fun of the prank to see all those letters flying out of the box.

If there were a TV show entitled "Stupid Stunts," those pranks just mentioned would get top billing. It is easy for the prank to get out of hand and turn into the sort of thing that ends up with someone injured, property damaged, and the pranksters standing before a judge in a hearing.

QUESTIONS

1. In the event a water balloon dropped from an apartment overhead or thrown from a speeding car results in serious injury, can the prankster be charged with the crime of battery? How about attempted murder? Why or why not might such charges be filed?

2. If stolen real estate or Neighborhood Watch signs are not damaged and can be used again, is it reasonable to charge the pranksters with even a misdemeanor? How might they better be punished?

3. Considering all fifty signs as one theft moves a prank into the felony category. Either support or oppose the legal thinking involved. (Remember New York City's graffiti policy.)

4. Mailbox bashing has to rate right at the top of really stupid pranks. In the case of destroying the mailbox and watching mail scatter, what additional problems may result if the box bashers are identified?

47. Stalking Isn't Love

Countless times for years on end, local police departments have received calls from frightened women. Their ex-husband, angry former boyfriend, or some unknown male has been following them, has been sending them letters and presents, or has made dozens or hundreds of phone calls at all hours of the day or night. Will the police please do something?

Until recently police almost always responded by asking if the follower, phone caller, or letter writer had harmed the frightened victim physically. If not, the police were unable to act. If death threats were made in writing, by phone, or verbally, the police might attempt to contact the person involved. Otherwise, it was a matter of waiting until the person harmed the victim and the police would then do something.

The police were not unsympathetic to the women, and a few males, who called. The police were bound by laws existing at that time, by laws that still exist in some locations.

In the 1980's and early 1990's, citizens, police, and lawmakers came to realize that stalking was serious. Time and time again a stalker became a rapist or a killer. Court orders to the contrary, many stalkers added physical harm to the mental harm they had already inflicted.

Currently antistalking laws have begun to address this problem. Public awareness of the danger stalkers posed to victims jolted some lawmakers into action. Serious penalties can be imposed upon individuals found guilty of stalking. Media photos of women lying dead in the street went a long way toward forcing some to realize stalking isn't just an expression of interest or love.

QUESTIONS

1. There is generally no minimum age at which a person can be charged with stalking. National attention focused on the elementary school boy charged under the stalking law because he continued to follow, write notes to, and generally annoy the elementary school girl of his dreams. Is an elementary school child actually capable of stalking? Why do you feel as you do?

_____

_____

2. At what point does a desire to be friends and be accepted cease being an attempt to express love and turn to stalking?

_____

_____

3. Courts can and do issue injunctions requiring a male considered dangerous to keep a certain distance from the female he is stalking. Many of the women who have received such protections are now dead, killed by the male against whom the injunction was issued. How can society better deal with this situation?

_____

_____

4. Most dangerous stalkers are male. Female stalkers usually don't cause physical harm. How does a male tell whether he may be in danger when he is stalked by a female? What recourse does he have in a society that is only gradually becoming aware that females are capable of crimes of violence?

---

48. Who Decides Whether It's Pornography on the Net or Web?

Anyone who has gone net surfing is likely to have discovered some sites out there that include extremely graphic sexual comment and illustrations.

In response to demands that Congress find a way to limit pornography available via computer, the Communications Decency Act was passed. From the moment President Clinton signed the CDA into law, critics said it was unconstitutional, a clear violation of the First Amendment. The CDA made it a criminal act to transmit "indecent" or "offensive" messages that minors might view. The problem is that "indecent" and "offensive" speech is protected by the First Amendment. Such messages are not the same as obscenity. July 1996 saw the death of the newly enacted law. Three judges said it was flawed and violated the standards of free speech.

The problem with protecting children and youths from messages, photos, and information available via computer is only somewhat similar to dealing with "adult" bookstores and magazines. First of all, *indecent, offensive,* and even *obscene* have different meanings for different people. Secondly, and more important, is the difficulty of limiting what comes via the computer to users of a given age. A local ordinance can deal with the age of patrons at the magazine shop or one section of the video store. Limiting computer access to users of a given age is just about impossible, especially as the average middle school student knows far more about computers than most parents do.

How do we regulate the exchange of messages among individuals of varying ages? Unfortunately, there are a number of people whose chat-room messages aren't what they appear to be. Some of those frequenting chat rooms are in reality in search of children and youths to victimize sexually. Most would agree that young people should not be made innocent victims of those who would exploit them sexually and otherwise.

In brief, the problem of porn via computer comes down to this: How do we regulate a means of communication vastly different from any form previously used? And, how do we provide necessary protection without violating the Constitution?

QUESTIONS
---

1. What constitutes a computer message that most of the members of your community would term "indecent" or "offensive"?

   _____

   _____

   _____

2. To you, personally, what is the difference between pornography and something that is indecent or offensive?

   _____

   _____

3. Congress and the president tried, and failed, to write a law that would protect children and youths from those who would use the computer to cause harm or victimize the young. You are probably more familiar with the computer than are most members of Congress and the president. What might be the solution to this problem? How can the net and Web be used by all without allowing some users to harm others, especially the young?

   _____

   _____

   _____

49. Potential Fraud Is Easy with Computers and Credit Cards

As you recall, fraud is a dishonest act or device designed to deprive a person of his or her rights or to harm a person. A host of schemes exist involving dishonest use of your credit card number.

All credit card holders are cautioned about giving their credit card number over the phone to someone they do not know. This, of course, does not mean you can't give your credit card number to the unknown clerk who needs your number to complete a telephone purchase of a catalog item. It does, however, mean that once an unknown caller obtains your credit card number, he or she can use it to charge to the limit of your card before you have any idea you are the victim of a fraud.

If someone does use your credit card number illegally, are you liable for the cost of goods purchased? No. The law protects you and leaves it up to the credit card company to help you straighten things out. It may take lots of your time, however, and you may learn your card is "maxed out" when you try to use it.

With the move toward using computers to make on-line purchases, the potential for illegal use of your credit card number has increased. Once your credit card number gets into the system, a hacker in cyberspace may put it to his or her own personal use. Again, the company backing the card is bound by law to help straighten things out, but it takes time and energy.

There is, however, a potential for future fraud in credit card and computer land that is, at present, totally legal. The key words here are *potential* and *future.*

Check your credit card. See that little magnetic strip? As you know, this contains information including your name and card number. That strip helps transmit the information so your credit card purchase can be approved. But that little magnetic strip is able to store and transmit an amazing amount of information about your buying habits. It can tell the credit card company where you shop, when you shop, and what sort of purchases you are likely to make. This information is, we are told, a marketing aid to help companies know what buyers wish them to sell. So far so good. There is nothing wrong with marketing surveys. Besides, this information has to be gathered in order for the credit card company to send your monthly bill.

Let's move on to Web sites. Does the term "Client-side persistent information" mean anything to you? Probably not. What this term means is that many web sites have a feature enabling them to gather and store information about your visit. Actually each site uses your hard drive to accomplish this. When your browsing takes you to a specific site again, the site is able to tell that you've been there before. This system also tells the site how long you were on site, where you went next, what sort of computer you have, and so on.

This is legal under current law. It is a marketing device enabling site owners to serve their visitors better. When this information is used along with other personal information, it allows site owners to know a tremendous amount about you. Can this lead to fraud? Not so long as the material gathered and stored is used simply to improve marketing. You may end up on a few mailing lists, but that's nothing new.

What troubles some is that citizens are totally unaware that this vast new information-gathering process is taking place. We have no control over how such information is used. We do not know who will be able to obtain such information. Perhaps worst of all is that there is currently no way to control the gathering and distribution of such information.

QUESTIONS

1. Is it an invasion of your privacy for companies to gather information about you when you use your credit card or visit a Web site? Or, since you made the purchase or visited the site, is this, in a sense, public information?

   _____

   _____

2. What possible future illegal uses can you see for information gathered from your use of credit cards or computers? _____

   _____

3. Is this really a problem? If so, what is the solution? If not, why not? _____

   _____

50. Flag Burning: A Form of Freedom of Speech

Most of us are totally turned off when we see a photo or TV clip of an individual or group burning the United States flag or trampling it underfoot. Flag burning stirs strong emotions. Some lawmakers have been so opposed to such activity that they have introduced legislation at federal, state, and even local levels to bar such activity and to make it a crime to burn or otherwise show lack of respect to the U.S. flag.

To the surprise of many and delight of some, the U.S. Supreme Court has ruled that burning, trampling, cutting, or otherwise damaging the U.S. flag is protected by the U.S. Constitution. The First Amendment of the Bill of Rights guarantees freedom of speech. The Supreme Court has ruled that flag burning is just another form of freedom of speech.

Since the Supreme Court has ruled in this manner, no state or city can enforce a law making flag burning a crime. Once the Supreme Court has made such a ruling, it requires a future Supreme Court ruling or an act of Congress to change things.

It was stated earlier that laws change as does society. Judges and courts interpret laws in a manner they feel is in keeping with modern life based upon past legal interpretations. The fact that those who wrote the Constitution could in no way envision what the future held and certainly could not predict the rulings of future courts is certainly obvious in the variety of court rulings regarding what constitutes freedom of speech.

QUESTIONS

1. The Supreme Court ruled that burning the United States flag is a form of freedom of speech. If someone opposed to flag burning threatens a flag burner, is that person also protected by the guarantee of freedom of speech?

   _____

2. In the event a flag burning gets out of control and the fire spreads, say to a building, is the flag burner guilty of arson, or is he or she protected because of freedom of speech guarantees?

   _____

3. Freedom of speech has come to include many things the Constitution writers never considered. A multitude of court rulings have confirmed that words, pictures, and acts offensive to many people are legal. What types of words, pictures, and actions would even the most liberal court not consider protected by the First Amendment?

   _____

   _____

51. Searches of Vehicles Require Probable Cause

It is quite common for a law enforcement officer to stop a vehicle for a traffic violation and realize something is wrong beyond just the traffic stop. Officers commonly ask the driver for permission to search the car. They may ask the driver to open the car's trunk to see what is inside. The officer may ask the driver to lift a blanket from the rear seat so whatever is covered becomes visible. At times traffic control officers have asked drivers and passengers to empty their pockets. Or they have asked to check beneath car seats, in glove boxes, and in door pockets.

The variety of illegal items found in such searches—dead bodies, kidnap victims, stolen goods, and illegal drugs, to name a few—indicates that many law enforcement officers have developed the ability to sense when something is wrong. This is based, at least in part, on the actions of the driver and/or passengers. It is sometimes based upon the time of day, the location of the traffic stop, past experience, and even the race of the driver.

Courts have ruled that law enforcement officials need probable cause to justify searching a car or asking for permission to search the car. Basing such a request upon the race of the car's occupants does not constitute probable cause to justify such a search. Using what is sometimes called a "profile," which includes past history of criminal activity in the area or along a particular highway, does not constitute probable cause.

In the thinking of our courts, stopping a driver for a traffic violation generally does not justify having the driver or passengers empty their pockets, open glove boxes, lift blankets, or open car trunks. This thinking is in keeping with constitutional protections safeguarding the rights of individuals.

Many times criminals have been set free because the courts ruled the evidence obtained was the result of a search without probable cause. In other cases judges have allowed evidence gathered after a traffic stop to be admitted because they felt the officer was in a position to see something that caused him or her to have probable cause for searching the vehicle.

In general, a traffic stop does not justify a search of the vehicle or its occupants. However, many citizens have a difficult time accepting the fact that a million dollars worth of illegal drugs or evidence of a murder cannot be used because the court decides an arresting officer lacked probable cause.

In protecting the rights of the innocent, our legal system sometimes allows the guilty to avoid punishment. It can be argued that protecting the rights of all citizens is more important than the fact that a few guilty individuals take advantage of the law.

QUESTIONS

1. An officer asks the driver to open the trunk of the car or the rear door of the van. As a result the officer discovers evidence of illegal activity and arrests the driver. Since the driver willingly opened the car's trunk or van's door, what does it matter why the officer first stopped the driver?

2. "Profiles" tell law enforcement officers that older cars, riding low on their springs, driven along a certain highway at 2:00 A.M. are likely to be carrying drugs. Our government wants to stop the illegal trade in drugs. If an officer stops a car that meets the profile and finds it is loaded with illegal drugs, why can't the courts accept this as probable cause for stopping the car?

_____

_____

3. "If you are innocent, you shouldn't mind if an officer asks to check the trunk of your car or wants you to move a blanket or open your glove compartment." React to this statement according to what you know about the law.

_____

_____

52. Drunkenness and the Influence of Drugs as a Defense

Defense attorneys have used drunkenness and the influence of drugs as a defense in criminal cases for many years. Their thinking goes something like this: My client was drunk, or my client was under the influence of drugs. Therefore my client had no true understanding of what he or she is accused of having done. Since my client had no understanding of the crime and can't recall having committed the crime, my client is innocent.

The legal basis for this defense is that a person who is drunk or under the influence of drugs is incapable of intending to commit a crime. This diminished capacity for intent makes them innocent of any crime committed while intoxicated.

The victims of crimes and surviving family members have always considered such a defense absurd. Someone went out, got drunk, took drugs, and then committed a crime ranging anywhere from assault to robbery to rape to murder. And now that "victim" wants society to believe he or she is not guilty.

The absolutely amazing thing is that this defense worked year after year in criminal cases all across the nation. Judges and juries listened

to defense attorneys and found their clients "not guilty" in case after case.

Prosecuting attorneys fought back by attempting to get state legislatures to pass laws prohibiting this sort of defense. By 1996 only ten states out of fifty had outlawed the "too drunk" defense. Then, in 1996 the U.S. Supreme Court ruled five to four that even though a man in Montana was legally drunk at the time he committed a felony, his conviction was correct. The surprising thing to many was that four members of the Supreme Court voted to accept the "too drunk" defense.

At any rate, this defense has now been overturned by the Supreme Court. Does this mean defense attorneys won't use the "too drunk" defense anymore? No, it does not. In the forty states that still allow this defense, attorneys will still attempt to use it as an excuse for their clients' crimes.

Only when state legislatures outlaw this form of defense will attorneys stop using it in a given state. Of course prosecutors will cite the Supreme Court decision to judges. However, many crimes are tried under state laws; therefore, each state must decide whether or not to pass legislation against the "too drunk" defense.

QUESTIONS

1. When a person chooses to drink alcohol or use drugs, is it not fair to assume this person has some idea as to what happens to the mental and physical ability of those who drink to excess or use drugs?

   _____

   _____

2. If the "too drunk" defense is valid, what other defenses might also be valid? (Recently "sugar high," "too much medication," and "I forgot to take my medication" have been in the news as criminal defenses.)

   _____

   _____

3. Consider the "too drunk" defense in criminal trials. What does accepting this defense suggest regarding the validity of drunk-driving laws?

   _____

   _____

53. The Battered-Wife Syndrome as a Defense

The "Case of the Burning Bed" brought home in graphic manner to the nation the problem of battered wives. There are no accurate statistics regarding the number of battered wives in the nation. This is because many cases of spousal abuse are never reported.

Only in fairly recent years did attorneys begin to successfully defend battered wives who finally struck back and killed their brutal husbands. This defense was based more on mental and emotional damage than on the actual physical harm suffered by the battered wife. Physical injuries and pain contribute to the mental and emotional damage. Defense attorneys have to convince juries that the battered wife was so brutalized both mentally and physically by her husband that she could

see no way out of the relationship except to kill him. Part of the defense relies on getting the jury to accept the fact the battered woman is so broken in spirit she can't simply walk away from her marriage. Her only solution is to end the battering by causing the death of her mate.

Prior to the acceptance of the battered-wife syndrome as a defense, a number of women had been convicted in the killing of husbands or live-in boyfriends. Once this defense was accepted as valid, the governors in several states pardoned dozens of women in prison for murder.

It has been argued that some women using this defense were not battered at all but have used this as a way to murder their husbands for insurance or whatever and escape punishment.

This is doubtlessly true. It is also true that numbers of wives have been beaten by their husbands to the point where they were emotionally and mentally incapable of escaping the situation.

Though some will abuse this defense, it is now a recognized defense and is a part of our legal system. This does not mean that every woman who pleads "not guilty" because she is a battered wife will be found innocent. It does indicate some women will be found innocent in the deaths of brutal men.

QUESTIONS

1. Why do some women allow their husbands or boyfriends to abuse them while others refuse to accept such brutality and get a divorce or end a relationship?

   _____

   _____

2. Why do so many battered women refuse to press charges against their husbands or boyfriends?

   _____

   _____

3. Many cities and states now require police to make an arrest in each and every instance officers are called to a domestic disturbance. The arrest is required whether the victim is willing to press charges or not. This policy appears to be successful in curbing domestic violence. What do you see as both positive and negative effects of such an arrest policy?

   _____

   _____

   _____

   _____

4. What do some women do that seems to deliberately cause the men in their lives to resort to some form of abuse? Why do these women do or say things they know from past experience will end in violence?

   _____

   _____

   _____

   _____

5. Only recently has society come to accept the fact that women can be mental and physical abusers just as men can. Why does our society make it so difficult for men to admit they are victims of

abuse? Why has our society historically insisted on harsher punishments for men than for women in so many instances?

_____

_____

_____

54. Same-Sex Marriages: Are They Coming to Your State?

The idea of same-sex marriages is not totally new. It came to the fore in the mid-1990's, when the state of Hawaii considered making such marriages legal. In 1996 the city of San Francisco held a large ceremony in which many same-sex unions were recognized by the city's mayor. At the time, members of Congress debated whether or not they should consider federal approval of same-sex marriages or if Congress should ban such unions.

While the question remains unanswered, as of this writing a number of cities and states throughout the nation are moving toward same-sex marriages. A major step in this direction is the fact that some cities and a number of corporations now provide health care for same-sex partners of municipal or corporate employees.

QUESTIONS

1. From a purely legal point of view, what are the advantages of allowing same-sex marriages? Consider the fact that countless same-sex couples have lived together sharing homes, incomes, and purchases for many years.

_____

_____

_____

2. Again, thinking only of legal complications, what are some problems likely to arise from recognizing same-sex marriages?

_____

_____

_____

55. Doctor-Assisted Suicide— Right or Wrong?

One of the promises a physician makes when he or she officially becomes a doctor is to do no harm. For centuries the majority of doctors have felt that to assist another person in dying violates this medical oath.

At the same time, there are a few doctors in the nation who have not found themselves unable to provide further medical help to a terminally ill patient. They, like the patient and the patient's family and friends, have been forced to watch long, painful deaths. Time and time again, dying patients have begged their doctors to speed them on their final journey.

It has long been considered a crime for a doctor to hasten the death of a patient. For this legal reason, if not for their medical oaths and personal moral reasons, doctors have been reluctant to assist in the death of a terminally ill patient. When the patient has suffered from a long, terribly painful death, this decision has seemed unjustly cruel to many.

Those who favor allowing doctors to assist in patient suicide point to the fact that the Netherlands has a doctor-assisted suicide law in place. There are numerous safeguards built in, so there is no danger a doctor will bring death to a patient unwilling to die.

The question of doctor-assisted suicide in the United States made national headlines when retired Dr. Jack Kevorkian began helping terminally ill patients die painlessly. Dr. Kevorkian made public his involvement in these suicides. Soon he was charged with a variety of crimes. By the fall of 1997, Dr. Kevorkian had never been convicted of a single crime. This, in itself, was an indication of a major change in the thinking of the American people.

The question did arise as to whether Dr. Kevorkian helped in the suicides of some individuals who were not terminally ill.

As debate over the actions of Dr. Kevorkian drew the attention of the media, a few physicians came forward and admitted they, too, had aided patients in achieving a painless death. A survey in which doctors could remain anonymous revealed that a number of doctors had done the same thing. Some doctors stated they believed this was medically and morally proper, even though they had not assisted anyone in dying. A number of church groups opposed any thought of doctor-assisted suicide.

In the meantime the voters of one state passed a law allowing doctors to assist in the suicide of a terminally ill patient. A neighboring state rejected the same law. Critics claimed this would endanger patients, despite protections for ill patients written into the law. No patient could be required to sign for assisted suicide. No one doctor could make the decision. A panel of doctors had to rule the patient had only a limited number of months yet to live. The patient had to be mentally competent.

To no one's surprise, an immediate court challenge was mounted when the doctor-assisted suicide law passed in one western state. The court found in favor of those who challenged the new law, and it was ruled invalid.

In the state of Washington, a law making doctor-assisted suicide a felony met with court challenges. One court ruled against the law in 1996. A higher court planned to review that ruling. Adding to the legal confusion was a federal appeals court decision striking down similar laws in seven western states.

Most states prosecute individuals who assist in the suicide of friends or loved ones. Critics of doctor-assisted suicides point to this fact and claim that doctors should be bound by the same laws as other citizens. Those who favor a law allowing doctors to end the suffering of the terminally ill counter by saying doctors are in a position to determine medically whether a person is facing death in the near future. Thus, they should be allowed to diminish suffering as an act of mercy.

QUESTIONS

1. It is not beyond possibility that a doctor, or even a panel of doctors, could be pressured or bribed into stating a patient's illness was terminal and then killing that person. Just how likely is this to occur?

   _____

   _____

2. In the event a doctor-assisted suicide law is passed and upheld by the courts, what sort of safeguards for both patient and doctor should be a part of that law?

   _____

   _____

   _____

3. What are some possible negative outcomes for doctors who are willing to ease suffering and assist in patient deaths once this action is made legal?

   _____

   _____

4. Should the patient's right to personal choice make a difference in this situation no matter what the law says? Why?

   _____

   _____

---

56. Recovered-Memory Accusations: Are They Real?

There is no question that laws and legal interpretations change as society changes.

Perhaps one of the most controversial changes in the way laws are applied has to do with so-called recovered- or repressed-memory accusations. A recovered-memory accusation comes as the result of someone suddenly recalling or claiming to recall that he or she witnessed a crime at some time in the past. These recovered memories or repressed memories come nearly always as the result of a series of sessions with a therapist.

One example illustrates how this works. A father was found guilty by a California jury in 1990 of having killed an eight-year-old girl in 1969. The witness against the father was his own daughter, who was twenty-nine years old at the time of the trial.

The defense claimed the daughter was hypnotized by her therapist and that the repressed memory was actually planted by suggestive questions. The daughter claimed she recalled yet another murder she saw her father commit. Fortunately for her father, DNA evidence proved he could not have committed the second murder. However, the man was convicted of the 1969 murder and imprisoned until a federal appeals court overturned the conviction in 1995.

It appears there is no doubt that repressed memories may surface years after an event. Psychologists tell us the shock of witnessing or being the victim of violent crime may cause the mind to block all memory of the event. Something may trigger recall years later.

For a time in the early 1990's, repressed-memory or recovered-memory trials took place in several states. A variety of crimes were recalled by witnesses whose therapists enabled them to remember the events. Some such crimes were murders. Others were rapes and assorted crimes of violence. Juries seemed willing to accept evidence offered by those whose memories returned. In one case the fact that the accused presented evidence he was in another state at the time of the crime made no difference. He, too, was found guilty.

There is no statute of limitations for the crime of murder. Thus there was no legal problem in bringing to trial those accused of murder. But in other crimes the statute of limitations does apply. How did prosecutors deal with the fact that a crime was supposedly committed twenty, thirty, or more years ago? The answer was simple. Courts accepted the idea that the statute of limitations began only when the repressed memory was recovered.

Critics of accepting recovered-memory evidence suggested therapists were planting such memories. Worse, it was possible for a person to provide such evidence as a means of harming or getting even with another individual.

Two events appear to have slowed the rush to prosecute these cases. One was the release of the California man charged by his daughter. A second was a court case in which a therapist was found guilty of implanting false memories in the mind of a patient.

Whether or not repressed- or recovered-memory cases will continue to be prosecuted remains to be seen. What is certain about those cases already tried is that they represent an instance of our legal thinking trying to adjust to the demands of society.

QUESTIONS

1. One of the major difficulties for a person accused of any crime twenty or thirty years in the past is presenting evidence of innocence. How might an accused person go about proving he or she could not have committed a crime that occurred in, say, 1970?

   _____

   _____

   _____

2. Therapists have a great deal of influence over their patients, who are generally suffering mental or emotional problems to begin with. These problems, of course, are what brings them to therapists for help. It is possible for therapists to influence patients improperly through repetition of certain suggestions. If such improper influence occurs, is the therapist guilty of a crime? If so, what is the crime?

3. What does our legal system need to do to protect innocent victims when accused of past crimes as a result of recovered or repressed memories?

4. What needs to be done to make certain that a legitimate recall of past evidence results in prosecution of the guilty?

57. Jury Nullification Lets the Guilty Go Free

Trial by jury is one of the basic rights we have as Americans. The entire thinking behind jury trials is that the accused is protected from false charges when a jury of his or her peers listens to the evidence.

Juries do make mistakes. All too often they are improperly influenced by clever arguments causing them to ignore the facts presented. However, by and large, the jury system has been successful and remains one of our extremely important basic rights.

In recent years the term *jury nullification* has been heard following a few trials.

Jury nullification simply means that a jury listens to the evidence presented and then ignores that evidence to return a verdict not supported by the evidence. It goes against all that our Constitution and Bill of Rights stand for. Historically, jury nullification was used by white juries to acquit a white person justly accused of having committed a crime against a black person. Or when a white jury found guilty a black person falsely accused of a crime against a white person.

In recent years jury nullification has been used in a few cases involving a member of a minority group accused of a crime. In these cases the jury has usually been composed largely of members of minority groups. Even though the evidence appears to point to the guilt of the person on trial, the jury has seemingly ignored that evidence and returned a verdict of "not guilty."

What makes jury nullification so surprising in today's world is that study after study indicates that jury members from the same minority group as the person on trial sometimes render harsher verdicts than do Anglo members when judging a minority person.

QUESTIONS

1. Why might minority jury members be more likely than Anglo members of the same jury to be harder on a minority member accused of a crime?

_____

_____

2. In certain instances, a judge is empowered to set aside the decision of a jury. This is rarely done. In the case of obvious jury nullification, why might a judge not set aside the jury's decision, even if he or she has the power to do so?

_____

_____

3. What might cause individual members of a jury to be willing to take part in jury nullification? Consider the fact that every jury member comes to a trial with his or her own background experiences.

_____

_____

58. School Busing for Racial Balance Was Not the Answer

In the years after the end of the Second World War, many of our cities experienced what came to be known as "white flight." Simply stated, this involved the movement of numbers of Anglo families from inner cities to the more spacious suburbs.

This reduced the ability of inner cities to raise taxes and created a situation where many schools were attended mostly by minority children. In all too many instances the schools attended by Anglo children tended to be newer, better equipped, and often better staffed than the schools attended mostly by minority children.

A court ruling in the 1960's ordered cities in the United States to bus students from one school to another in order to achieve racial balance in the public schools. This was an instance of a member of the judicial branch of government making a law by a court ruling.

As a result of this ruling, millions of schoolchildren were bused from their neighborhood schools to schools in another part of the city. The idea behind the ruling, of course, was that if the same percentage of white children and of minority children were present in every school, then all schools would provide equal educational opportunities for all children.

School busing for racial balance became commonplace and was eventually widely accepted, though it was expensive and caused countless children as young as five years of age to spend large amounts of time riding school buses.

By the mid-1990's, a number of school districts appealed to the courts for permission to end school busing based strictly on racial numbers. In some cities judges ruled the school board had done everything possible to achieve equality in education and allowed a gradual lessening of busing for racial balance. This change in policy was welcomed by many parents and their children, regardless of race. To them it seemed entirely illogical to force a child to ride a bus for forty-five minutes or an hour each morning and afternoon when a school stood sometimes next door to the child's home.

Once again, both the beginning and the gradual ending of school busing for racial balance illustrate the attempts of the law to meet the needs of our society.

QUESTIONS

1. Under our Constitution, Congress and state legislatures are given the job of passing laws. The judicial branch or court system is supposed to interpret these laws and, at times, decide whether a law is constitutional. At times, as in the case of school busing, judges and courts impose rulings that actually have the force of law. Why is this right, or why is it wrong?

_____

_____

_____

2. In what ways was the nation different in the mid-1990's than it was in the 1960's when busing for racial balance came into being? What had changed in a quarter of a century that might have influenced judges to be willing to allow a city to end school busing?

_____

_____

59. Gerrymandering Was Wrong in 1811 and in 1996

Elbridge Gerry was governor of Massachusetts in 1810 and 1811. He devised a scheme enabling members of the political party in power to remain in power at the next election. What Governor Gerry put into being was a redrawing of the lines for political districts so that his party's voters had a majority in most districts. In this way a district, 90 percent of whose voters supported his party, was divided so that some of those voters were moved to other voting districts. Now instead of having two or three districts with huge majorities in his party while seven or eight districts provided the other party with a slight majority, Gerry created many districts in which his party members enjoyed a slight majority. This left opposing parties controlling no districts or just a few.

The plan came to be known as "gerrymandering." The voting districts had strange shapes as the lines were redrawn along party lines rather than geographic lines.

The U.S. Supreme Court ruled this sort of redrawing of voting lines unconstitutional, and Gerry's plan failed. However, anytime voting lines are redrawn, they are still likely to be redrawn to the advantage of the political party in power at the time.

By the end of the 1980's, a new form of gerrymandering came into use in congressional elections. A number of voting districts were redrawn in strange shapes so that African-American and Latino political candidates would be all but assured of election to Congress. As a result of these redrawn congressional districts, the number of African American and Latino members in Congress increased.

However, the Supreme Court ruled that redrawing voting districts based entirely on race was unconstitutional. The court ruled that voting districts had to be race neutral. In other words, it is against the law to deliberately draw a voting district based entirely upon the race of the people living in the area. Just as it had once been ruled that political gerrymandering was unconstitutional, it was now ruled that racial gerrymandering is also against the law.

Some civil rights advocates opposed this ruling. They claimed it was a blow to equal representation. At the same time, political analysts said few minority members of Congress risked losing their seats.

It is interesting to note that in several primary elections in the summer of 1996 in districts changed by the court ruling, the minority members seeking re-election won the right to represent their party in the November elections.

QUESTIONS

1. Some people argue that racial gerrymandering is acceptable in order to achieve a better racial balance in Congress. Why is this argument right or wrong?

_____

_____

2. When the Supreme Court voted against racial gerrymandering, the vote was five to four. What does this tell us?

_____

_____

60. Affirmative Action Is Questioned

Affirmative action is a process that has required the setting of racial quotas in an effort to achieve racial balance in a number of areas. Such quotas were intended to make up, at least in part, for past injustices suffered by some minority groups.

One area in which affirmative action was put to use involved the hiring of labor by contractors working for the government. In these situations a certain percentage of all workers hired by the contractor had to come from minority groups. Otherwise the contractor could not work for the government.

In many areas of government including state and local government, job quotas were established to guarantee that a certain percentage of all newly hired workers would be from minority populations. In order to achieve the quotas set, it was often necessary to overlook qualified Anglo workers in order to promote minority workers. In the case of certain civil-service examinations for hiring, a given number of points was automatically added to the test scores of minority members.

In many cities promotion in certain jobs, such as police and fire departments, was based on the quota system. Since it was common to have few, if any, minority members in some of these departments in administrative positions, quotas were set requiring that future promotions be made from among the ranks of minority members of the department.

To be eligible to sell their products to the government, manufacturers of some products had to abide by racial quotas among their workers.

Affirmative action requirements were extended to include women. Though women actually constitute a majority of the nation's population, they were considered a minority group under affirmative action because they had been discriminated against in many situations in past years.

When government contracts were let at all levels of government, a certain percentage of businesses receiving contracts had to be owned by minority members or women.

Anglo men who were denied promotion, whose companies were denied government contracts even when they were a low bidder on the project, and who were not hired despite high test scores and adequate qualifications began to file reverse discrimination suits in court. They claimed they were being discriminated against in favor of minority members and women. Courts began to rule in favor of Anglo men in these reverse discrimination suits. Anglo women brought suit in cases when they were fired or not promoted because the job or promotion was awarded a minority woman. By the middle of the 1990's, the Supreme Court ruled that it was wrong to discriminate against anyone in order to achieve racial quotas.

The interesting thing concerning the setting of all racial quotas is that this is specifically forbidden by the 1964 Civil Rights Act. This act states that it is illegal to discriminate in employment on the basis of "race, color, religion, sex, or national origin." In other words, any quota set to advance members of one race or either sex over other members of our society is against federal law.

So how did the federal government go about setting quota systems to further affirmative action? It was done in part by presidential proclamation. Presidents often issue proclamations (which are really edicts) to accomplish some goal. In the case of racial and sexual quotas, the nation accepted such proclamations despite the fact that they were clearly against the law. Congress also passed laws supporting quotas based on race and sex. The courts allowed such laws to stand.

One goal of our nation's legal system is to have a color-blind society. In an attempt to create racial equality, affirmative action created a form of racial discrimination moving in a direction opposite that of reaching a truly color-blind society.

QUESTIONS

1. Is it possible to make up for past injustices that occurred generations ago?

   _____

2. What approach might be better than setting racial quotas when it comes to achieving a color-blind system of hiring and promotion?

   _____

   _____

   _____

3. When rules designed to aid minority members were employed to help advance women, people began to speak of minorities and women to deal with the fact that women are not a minority in our nation. Support or oppose extending racial quotas and affirmative action to cover women.

_____

_____

_____

4. Why did it take so many years for the courts to begin to rule that racial quotas were discriminatory and in violation of the 1964 Civil Rights Act?

_____

_____

61. Some Groups Don't Recognize Government Authority

Events in the 1990's called the nation's attention to the fact that "patriot" groups within the United States did not recognize the authority of the government at any level.

Members of these groups refused to license their vehicles, refused to get driver's licenses, failed to pay taxes, and claimed U.S. currency had no value.

In some instances certain members of such groups attempted to pay off loans with no-account checks they claimed represented their right to coin their own money. Some groups filed false property liens against government officials who did not agree with their thinking.

At the same time that these individuals claimed the government had no authority to regulate their actions, they used highways paid for from government funds, accepted United States currency in payment for goods and services, and in some cases accepted government funds for such things as farm guarantees.

The appeal of such groups was obvious. The thought of having all the benefits and none of the legal responsibilities of citizenship caused many to join. The question is, of course, how far can government allow individuals to go before our legal system breaks down?

QUESTIONS

1. How far should governments at any level go in allowing individuals and groups to violate the rules under which their neighbors and fellow citizens live?

_____

_____

2. Members of some groups borrowed money from lending institutions and individuals and then "repaid" it by writing no-account checks they said were drawn on their own monetary system. What recourse do the institutions and individuals have in such cases?

_____

_____

3. Distrust of our present government is the basis for many of the groups formed. What things about the way our government currently operates would cause many citizens to mistrust their government?

_____

_____

_____

4. What should be done to enforce laws covering such things as vehicle licensing, driver's licenses, payment of taxes, repayment of debt, etc.?

_____

_____

Final Quiz

1. The neighborhood bully recently injured three citizens in separate attacks. Two victims are in the hospital. Seven witnesses identified the bully as the attacker.

   Which of the following are correct in this case?

   (a) _____ The bully most likely committed criminal acts.

   (b) _____ The Code Of Hammurabi may apply to the bully.

   (c) _____ The bully is probably guilty of battery.

   (d) _____ Any state or local laws used to charge the bully must agree with the United States Constitution.

   (e) _____ If the bully is charged by the district attorney, this will be a civil case.

2. The Slick and Slime Company sold a physical-fitness device for a high price. Slick and Slime said it was guaranteed to improve fitness. Jennifer bought the product and began to use it. Two days later the device broke, causing Jennifer to fall and injure herself. Slick and Slime told Jennifer it has no liability. Later, Jennifer went to her attorney.

   What might her attorney have told Jennifer in this case?

   (a) _____ Slick and Slime is guilty of libel.

   (b) _____ This case will be tried in civil court.

   (c) _____ This problem is one called a tort.

   (d) _____ If Jennifer sues Slick and Slime, she will be a plaintiff.

   (e) _____ It will be up to Slick and Slime to file a complaint.

3. When Bob sold his used riding mower to Ted, it seemed to Ted that he got a bargain. Soon after paying for the mower, Ted found that it did not run well. Then it did not run at all. Ted took it to the repair shop. An employee recognized the mower and told Ted that it was not worth repairing. Bob refused to refund Ted's money. Ted can't afford to hire a lawyer.

Which are true facts regarding Ted's problems?

(a) _____ Ted may go to small claims court.

(b) _____ Since Ted can't afford a lawyer, he is entitled to a public defender's services.

(c) _____ Bob is probably guilty of extortion.

(d) _____ If Ted threatens to hit Bob with a baseball bat, Ted will be guilty of assault even if he does not actually hit Bob.

(e) _____ If Ted takes this case to county civil court or small claims court, the court clerk can act as Ted's attorney for a small fee.

4. Flashing red lights indicated that the police officer wanted the motorist to pull over. The driver stopped and waited for the officer to leave her patrol car.

"What did I do, Officer?" the driver asked.

"You made an improper turn," she replied. "You turned right at the red light when a pedestrian was crossing."

"I'm from out of town," the driver protested. "I didn't know I was doing something wrong."

What legal principles seem to apply in this case?

(a) _____ The right-turn law is an edict.

(b) _____ Unless the right-turn law is part of common law, it cannot be enforced.

(c) _____ Ignorance of the right-turn law is not considered an excuse for breaking the law.

(d) _____ The motorist may end up charged with committing a tort.

(e) _____ If the driver goes to court, he will be a defendant.

5. Jason is thirteen years old but spends lots of time with his older brother and his brother's friends. Jason is friendly and well liked. He is also loyal to his brother. When Jason's brother got into a fight with three other fellows, Jason joined in. He was doing well for himself when the police arrived. All five of the combatants were loaded into patrol cars.

What is likely to happen because the police are involved?

(a) _____ Jason will be booked and fingerprinted.

(b) _____ If Jason is charged, he will have a hearing instead of a trial.

(c) _____ Jason will probably be released to his parents instead of being held in jail.

(d) _____ Since older youths were involved, Jason will be tried as an adult.

(e) _____ Jason's name will probably appear in the local newspaper in the police log section.

6. Sue and Jessica did not consider what they did to be a crime. It was just that they wanted to have nice things they could not afford. For years the two had helped themselves to costume jewelery, cosmetics, and other small items displayed in department stores. Recently their shoplifting had expanded to include expensive clothing. Today store detectives detained them. Police officers arrived and arrested them. Then the two police officers took them out of the department store.

Which of these statements apply to Sue and Jessica?

(a) _____ They have certain protections granted by the Constitution.

(b) _____ Since they are high school students, the Miranda warning does not apply.

(c) _____ They must use their right to one phone call to contact an attorney.

(d) _____ A lawyer will have to get a writ of *habeas corpus* in order to get Sue and Jessica out of jail.

(e) _____ If the girls have to appear in court, they will be charged in a civil court because they are under eighteen years of age.

7. Bad Bob grew up as a gang member. He moved on to dealing drugs and holding up convenience stores. Bad Bob has been in and out of police stations for years but somehow always managed to avoid going to prison. Now, at the age of twenty-two, Bob is in real trouble. He beat up a store clerk during a holdup. A priest saw the event and is a witness at Bob's trial.

What can be said about Bob's situation?

(a) _____ Since the clerk did not die, Bob did not commit a felony.

(b) _____ Even though the priest identified him, Bob is still presumed innocent when the trial begins.

(c) _____ Bob's lawyer can cross-examine the priest, even though everyone knows the priest is telling the truth.

(d) _____ Bob cannot be required to testify at the trial.

(e) _____ If Bob takes the witness stand, the prosecuting attorney cannot ask questions that might cause Bob to incriminate himself.

8. The neighbors decided enough was enough. It was bad having a crack house down the street. It was worse that the police seemed unwilling to deal with the problem. After one of the drug dealers attacked several neighborhood girls, a large group of angry residents decided to solve the problem. They armed themselves and started toward the crack house.

Which of the following are true statements?

(a) _____ If the neighbors burn the crack house, they can't be charged with arson because the crack house is illegal.

(b) _____ The neighbors can plead self-defense because they are protecting themselves and others from the drug dealers.

(c) _____ If police order the neighbors to leave the crack house, it is a lawful order that must be obeyed even though the drug dealers are criminals.

(d) _____ If angry neighbors take items by force from a store that sells groceries to the drug dealers, they are guilty of looting.

(e) _____ When a crack dealer was killed by a shot fired from the crowd, the death was a homicide even though no one knew who fired the shot.

9. Larry and Tami hit upon a plan to make some quick money. They would volunteer to help old Mrs. Johnson clean her house. While they cleaned, they would steal anything of value they saw. Mrs. Johnson was nearly blind, so this would be easy. They told Sally about their plan, but Sally did not help them. After they stole from Mrs. Johnson, they told Fred what they had done. Neither Sally nor Fred reported their friends.

What describes the legal state of affairs at this point?

(a) _____ Sally is an accessory before the fact.

(b) _____ Fred is not an accessory.

(c) _____ Larry and Tami are guilty of conspiracy.

(d) _____ Larry and Tami committed robbery.

(e) _____ Larry and Tami may be guilty of fraud.

10. It was one of those spring days when it was too nice to go to school. Evan, Troy, and Michelle took the afternoon off to hang out. They picked up some picnic supplies and headed out in Troy's car. They parked in a private drive and had their picnic on private land without asking permission. Later in the day Michelle spray painted their names on the side of a garage. To end their day Evan used his fake I.D. to buy a couple of six-packs of beer.

What is their legal situation by day's end?

(a) _____ They are guilty of trespass.

(b) _____ They committed several felonies.

(c) _____ Michelle is guilty of larceny.

(d) _____ They are habitual truants who violated the state compulsory attendance law.

(e) _____ Evan is guilty of entrapment.

11. Sara was sick and tired of the way Kati kept making jokes about Sara and her boyfriend. She decided it was time to pay Kati back. Sara printed a bunch of flyers calling Kati a liar. Sara also drew a cartoon showing Kati with both feet in her mouth and a bottle of whiskey in her hand. For good measure Sara reworked Kati's yearbook photo so Kati looked terrible.

Of what offenses is Sara probably guilty?

(a) _____ Sara committed libel.

(b) _____ Sara broke the copyright law.

(c) _____ Kati was slandered by the flyers and cartoon.

(d) _____ Sara defamed Kati.

(e) _____ Sara has menaced Kati.

12. What began as a night out with friends turned into a nightmare for Kevin. Joleen had her parents' new car and wanted to show off. Carol brought along beer for everyone. Larry saw Jerrod's car and used a screwdriver to cut grooves in the paint. Carol drank too much and began throwing food at customers in a fast-food spot. Joleen and Kevin both used the steps of the library as a toilet. Joleen hit sixty-five in a twenty mile-per-hour zone as they left the library.

Which of the following did one or more of the group commit?

(a) _____ Vandalism

(b) _____ Disturbing the peace

(c) _____ Eluding

(d) _____ Disorderly conduct

(e) _____ Menacing

13. Charlie and Pete were playing a little one-on-one as they had at the outdoor court every day for the past month. When Pete scored again, Charlie shoved him hard out of frustration.

"Watch it!" Pete snarled.

"Or what?" Charlie shoved Pete hard in the chest.

"Or I'll break your stupid face!" Pete shouted. "I'll put you in intensive care!"

Charlie hit Pete in the nose. Blood flew. Then Charlie grabbed a chunk of two-by-four lying at the edge of the ball court and swung it. The board caught Pete in the ribs.

What is the legal situation for the two basketball players?

(a) _____ Pete committed assault.

(b) _____ Charlie is guilty of battery.

(c) _____ Charlie committed an aggravated assault.

(d) _____ Pete is guilty of negligence.

(e) _____ Charlie can be charged with perjury.

14. The Hang Out was known as a tough bar. Tiger Joe, the owner, kept order with a baseball bat when necessary. When Dave had too much to drink, Tiger refused to serve him. Dave protested, and Tiger told him to leave.

    "I'll kill you!" Dave yelled as he left the Hang Out.

    Five minutes later Dave returned carrying a shotgun. He raised the weapon and fired twice at Tiger Joe. The bar owner was dead before he fell to the floor.

    What is Dave's legal position?

    (a) _____ He will be charged with carrying a concealed weapon.

    (b) _____ Dave committed aggravated assault.

    (c) _____ Dave is guilty of homicide.

    (d) _____ Dave committed justifiable homicide.

    (e) _____ Dave's crime is a felony.

15. Jim made a career of crime. When Alyce told him she wanted a new CD player but could not afford it, Jim told her he could get one cheap. That night Jim pried open a rear window at Sound Buy and grabbed a CD player. While he was at it, Jim also stole a dozen CDs. The next day he sold the CD player to Alyce for $20 and both of them were pleased.

    Where do things stand for Jim and Alyce?

    (a) _____ Jim is guilty of larceny.

    (b) _____ Jim committed burglary.

    (c) _____ Jim is guilty of robbery.

    (d) _____ Alyce can be charged with possession of stolen property even though she did not know Jim stole the CD player.

    (e) _____ Alyce is an accessory to Jim's crime.

Glossary

Accessory—A person who knows about a crime even though he was not present when the crime was committed. One who either helps plan a crime or conceals evidence of the crime after it was committed.

Action—A court procedure to enforce a right, prevent a wrong, or punish one who broke the law.

Adoption—Legally taking another person's child into your own family and treating him or her as your own.

Adult—One who has reached the age of majority or legal responsibility. A person who is no longer a minor.

Affidavit—A sworn written statement made before a person authorized to administer oaths.

Age of majority—Age at which one becomes legally able to act for him or herself as an adult.

Agent—One who is given authority to act for another person.

Aggravated assault—Deliberate violence against a person. Usually a dangerous weapon is involved, or another crime is also intended.

Alias—An assumed name.

Alibi—Fact or proof that one was not at the scene of a crime when it was committed.

Alien—A person living in one country who is a citizen of another.

Alimony—Money that a spouse (usually a husband) must pay for the support of the other spouse (usually a wife) after a divorce, separation, or annulment.

Annulment—A decision by a court that a marriage is null and no longer in effect.

Answer—The written reply of the defendant in a court case.

Appeal—A court procedure in which a case is taken before a higher court so that the court may review the decision of a lower court.

Appear—To come before the court as a party to a legal action or suit.

Apprehend—To capture or arrest a person accused of having committed a crime.

Arraignment—A procedure in which a person accused of a crime is brought to court to hear the charges against him or her, and to plead either guilty or not guilty to the charges.

Arrest—Use of legal authority to hold or to stop a person or to take away a person's freedom of movement.

Arson—Intentional burning of a house or other building, or having such a building burned.

Assault—An attempt or threat to cause physical harm to another.

Assault and battery—Carrying out an act of violence against another person after having threatened to do so.

Assault with a deadly weapon—Threatening or causing injury with a weapon likely to cause death or great bodily harm.

Asset—Property a person owns that may be used to pay debts.

Assign—To endorse over to another person, as a check.

Attractive nuisance—A hazard that a property owner knows about and knows is likely to attract children and result in their injury.

Award—The decision of a court granting money to the winner of a suit.

Bail—Money or security put up or pledged for the release from jail of a person accused of a crime. The released person promises to return for trial when called, or the money or security is turned over to the court.

Bail bond—A note signed by one accused of a crime that guarantees he will appear in court at a certain time.

Bankruptcy—A federal court procedure that helps people or companies unable to pay bills and debts as they come due.

Battery—An unlawful physical injury done to a person.

Bench warrant—A document issued by a court for the arrest of a person. Often used when the accused does not appear for trial.

Bequeath—To leave property to someone in a will.

Bigamy—Being married to more than one person at a time.

Bill of attainder—Any law that takes away a person's property. Such a law is illegal under the provisions of the Constitution.

Bill of sale—A document transferring ownership of personal property.

Bookmaking—Taking bets or wagers in a place not specified by law.

Breach of promise—Failure to keep one's promise in an important matter, such as not keeping a promise to marry someone.

Breach of the peace—Any act committed by a person in a public place that disturbs the public peace.

Breaking and entering—Breaking a door or window or picking a lock to go into a building the person has no legal right to enter.

Bribery—Paying a person to change her mind or to get her to act illegally.

Burden of proof—The legal need to prove facts in order to win a case in court. In criminal cases, the burden of proof is on the prosecution.

Burglary—A crime committed when a person breaks into the home or building of another with the intention of committing a crime.

Case—An action or suit brought before the court.

Caveat emptor—A principle in commerce that translates as "Let the buyer beware."

Charge—An accusation against a person saying that he has committed a crime. In legal cases, the charge is the set of instructions that the court gives the jury, explaining the law at the end of the trial.

Chattel—Personal property.

Child Abuse—Harm done to children by adults.

Circumstantial evidence—Known facts having to do indirectly with the question before the court. From these facts, a reasonable person can draw conclusions as to the correctness of other facts.

Civil action—A court action or case between individuals, not a criminal case.

Civil courts—Courts in which civil actions or trials are decided.

Civil law—The law covering civil or private actions. Used in France and some other European countries and the state of Louisiana, this type of law grew out of the old Roman law.

Code—A written collection of laws.

Collusion—A secret agreement, act, or conspiracy to defraud another person or to take part in an unlawful act.

Common law—Laws that are based on years of use and that resulted from previous court decisions. This system of law came from England.

Common-law marriage—An agreement of marriage between a couple, but without the marriage ceremony or legal paperwork.

Compensatory damages—Money awarded the plaintiff in a trial to make up for an injury to his person, reputation, or property.

Complaint—A document in which the plaintiff in a lawsuit outlines his claims for damages against the defendant.

Compulsory attendance laws—Laws that require minors below a certain age to attend school for a certain number of days each year.

Concealed weapon—A weapon such as a gun or knife carried so it is hidden from view. A penknife is not normally considered a concealed weapon.

Confession—An admission that one is guilty of the crime with which he is charged.

Consideration—Something of value offered to persuade a person to enter into a valid contract.

Conspiracy—An agreement between two or more people to commit an illegal act.

Contempt—Disregard for the authority of a court or a refusal to obey the orders of a court.

Contract—A legally binding agreement between two or more persons or companies.

Conviction—The decision of a court that a person accused of a criminal act is guilty.

Copyright—A law that grants writers and publishers the exclusive right to print and sell a written work for a certain number of years.

Corporal punishment—Physical punishment.

Corpus delicti—Evidence that proves a crime was committed, as in the finding of a body.

Creditor—A person to whom a debt is owed.

Crime—A wrong against the public, an act against the state, or an act for which one may go to jail or prison.

Criminal courts—Courts that hear cases dealing with criminal acts or violations of criminal law.

Cross-examination—The questioning of an opposing witness in court.

Damages—Money that the court says one person must pay to another because of harm caused by acts or failure to act when necessary.

Deadly force—Any force that can cause death or serious harm to another person.

Debtor—A person who owes money.

Decision—A court judgment.

Decree—A decision by a court.

Deed—A written document transferring the ownership of land from one person to another.

Defamation—Harming another person's character or reputation by saying things that aren't true and that are intended to bring harm.

Default—Failure to appear in court to defend against a lawsuit.

Defendant—The person who is accused of a crime in a criminal case, or the person sued in a civil case.

Defense—The things said and done for the defendant so that he or she will not have to lose freedom or pay damages.

Delinquent—A minor who commits a crime or is beyond parental control.

Deposition—A written statement made under oath. This may be used in court rather than having the person testify.

Dismiss—Throw a case out of court.

Disorderly conduct—Any acts that disturb the peace or are offensive to the morals of the public.

Disturbing the peace—Doing things that interrupt or disturb the peace and quiet of the community.

Divorce—Ending a marriage with the help of the court.

Domicile—The home of a person.

Donor—One who makes a gift.

Double jeopardy—Having to run the risk of paying the penalty for the same crime more than once.

Due process of law—Following legal procedure before taking away the life, liberty, or property of anyone.

Duress—Force or threats that cause a person to do something he does not wish to do.

Edict—Any law made by the ruler of a country.

Eluding—Fleeing police or other law officers in an effort to avoid capture; generally associated with vehicles.

Emancipation of a minor—A legal decision to allow a minor to carry on business as an adult.

Embezzlement—Stealing personal property that the owner has entrusted to another's care.

Enjoin—To forbid.

Enticement—Convincing a person to commit an unlawful or harmful act.

Entrapment—The process by which a law enforcement officer induces a person to commit a crime so that the officer can arrest him.

Error—A mistake in the way the law was used or applied. An error makes it possible to grant an appeal by a higher court.

Evict—To make someone give up his or her right to stay on and use a piece of property.

Ex post facto—A law passed that applies to acts committed before the law became a law. Such laws cannot be used against people.

Exemplary damages—Damages that are more than the actual damages. An increase in damages due to violence or fraud.

Exhibits—Documents or physical evidence used in a trial.

Expert witness—A witness in a trial who is qualified because of experience or education in a specific subject.

Extortion—Taking money or property away from a person by threat or duress.

False arrest—An unlawful arrest or taking away of a person's liberty.

Felony—A serious crime that may bring punishment of a year or more in prison.

Foreclosure—The sale of property to cover an unpaid debt secured or covered by the property.

Forgery—Falsely writing or changing a written item with the intent to defraud.

Fraud—A dishonest act or device used to deprive another of his rights or to harm another.

Grand jury—A special group of citizens that has the power to investigate possible criminal acts and to indict people accused of crimes after determining such people should stand trial.

Guardian—A person made legally responsible for taking care of another person who is usually a minor or someone unable to handle his or her own affairs.

Habeas corpus—An order granted by a court that requires a prisoner be brought to court so the court can decide whether it is legal to keep that person prisoner.

Habitual truant—A minor who does not regularly attend school even though required to do so by law.

Hearing—Not a trial but a less formal checking of issues by a judge or other government agency.

Hearsay—Information that one person got from another without knowing for sure whether it is absolutely correct.

Heir—One who inherits property.

Homicide—The killing of a person.

Illegitimate child—A child born to parents who are not married to each other.

Immunity—A guarantee by the court that a person will not be prosecuted in return for giving criminal evidence against another person.

In loco parentis—Meaning "in the place of the parents," and describing the rights and position of teachers, for example.

Incompetent—One who can't manage his or her affairs because of mental inability, insanity, or other handicap.

Indictment—A formal accusation made by a grand jury when it accuses someone of having committed a crime.

Infant—A minor; one under legal age.

Inheritance—Property, goods, or money received from a person upon his death.

Injunction—A court order demanding that a person do something or stop doing something.

Inquest—An inquiry or hearing concerning the manner of death of someone who dies suddenly.

Insolvent—Unable to pay one's debts.

Instrument—A written document.

Judge—A public official who is elected or appointed to preside over a court of law.

Judgment—A court decision.

Jurisdiction—The area or subjects over which a certain court has authority.

Jury—A group of citizens chosen to listen to evidence in court and decide a case.

Jury nullification—When a jury disregards evidence of guilt presented in a trial and finds the accused not guilty.

Juvenile courts—Courts with the power to judge cases dealing with young people.

Kidnapping—Taking and holding a person against his or her will for an illegal purpose, such as for payment of ransom.

Landlord—A person who rents property to another person.

Larceny—The illegal seizure of another's property; theft, stealing.

Legal duty—Something a person is required to do or not do because of the law.

Liability—Legal responsibility to make a payment or other amends for something wrong that has been done.

Libel—Publication of written or drawn items that are intended to hurt the reputation of a person.

License—Legal permission to do something that would be against the law without the license.

Litigation—Carrying on a lawsuit to enforce a right.

Majority—The age at which a young person legally becomes an adult.

Malice—Intent to do something that would harm another without cause.

Malicious mischief—Willful destruction of personal property.

Manslaughter—The killing of another person without malice. Voluntary manslaughter comes as the result of the heat of passion, and involuntary manslaughter is the accidental result of a careless or illegal act.

Menace—To use threats to force a person to enter into a contract.

Minor—One who has not yet reached the age of majority or adulthood.

Misdemeanor—A crime less serious than a felony and which may be punished by fine or jail or both.

Misrepresentation—A false statement made in order to deceive another.

Mortgage—A pledge of property to guarantee payment of a loan.

Murder—An unlawful killing of a person, with malice.

Negligence—Failure to use reasonable care. Carelessness that results in legal liability.

Nuisance—An act or use of property that annoys or inconveniences others, damages property, or keeps others from using and enjoying property.

Offense—A violation of a local ordinance or regulation, not a crime.

Opinion—A court's decision in a case.

Oral—Verbal or spoken, as in an oral contract.

Ordinance—A law written for a city or town.

Pardon—Made by the governor of a state or the president, it releases a convicted person from the punishment set by a court.

Parental liability—A law making parents legally responsible and liable for malicious damage caused by their children.

Perjury—The crime of making an untrue statement deliberately while under oath.

Personal property—Items such as cars, furniture, clothing, jewelry, and stocks and bonds, which may be easily moved.

Petition—A written request for legal relief filed in court by the party bringing suit against another.

Plaintiff—The person who brings or starts a lawsuit.

Plea—Answer made in court by the person accused of a crime.

Plea bargain—Allowing an accused person to plead guilty to some charges or to lesser charges in return for the government's promise to drop other charges.

Police power—The power of the government to pass laws and act to protect people.

Power of attorney—Written authority given by a person to have another act for him or her.

Precedent—Previous court decisions that other courts may follow in related cases.

Premeditation—Plotting; considering an act before taking action; deciding ahead of time to act.

Prima facie evidence—Strong evidence that is considered correct unless it can be proven wrong.

Privileged communication—Statement made to a lawyer, doctor, or priest, that may not be repeated without permission of the one making the statement.

Probable cause—A reasonable basis for supposing that a criminal charge is true.

Probate court—A court that deals with wills and estates.

Probation—A sentence that allows a person found guilty of a crime to stay out of prison in return for good behavior.

Prosecution—The legal agency or person conducting a suit against a person accused of a crime.

Public defender—An attorney appointed by the court to defend a person who is unable to hire his own lawyer.

Public interest—The well-being of the community or of the people.

Public nuisance—Activity that offends, endangers, or obstructs a number of people.

Punitive damages—Damages awarded to punish a person for violence, malice, or fraud.

Rape—Having sexual intercourse with a person as the result of using force or the threat of force or harm.

Real property—Owned land and whatever is built or growing on it.

Reprieve—A temporary suspension of the death sentence.

Rescind—To cancel.

Right to privacy—The right of a person to keep himself and his property out of public view.

Robbery—The forcible taking of personal property or money by use of violence or the threat of violence.

Search warrant—An order issued by a judge, which allows a law officer to search certain premises.

Self defense—Protection of one's person or property against harm from another.

Sentence—Punishment set by a court for a person found guilty of a crime.

Settlement—An agreement that settles a dispute without a court decision.

Sex assault on a child—Having sexual intercourse with a child.

Shoplifting—Removing goods from a store without paying for them.

Slander—Saying false things about another person in public. Saying false things that may hurt a person's reputation.

Spouse—Husband or wife.

Squatter—A person who takes over land without having title to it.

Statute—A law passed by a legislature.

Statute of limitations—Law that set limits to the time within which legal action can be brought as the result of acts committed.

Subpoena—A legal order requiring a person to appear in court.

Summons—Notice that legal action has been started and that a person is required to appear in court on a certain date.

Tenant—A person who pays rent for the use of land or buildings belonging to another person.

Testify—Give evidence at a trial or hearing.

Title—Ownership; a person's right to property.

Tort—Violation of law that causes injury to another person or his property. This is a civil wrong, not a crime.

Transcript—A written record of all that is said during a trial, hearing, or deposition.

Treasure trove—Money, coins, gold, jewels, or other treasure found with no way to locate the rightful owner.

Trespass—Unlawful entry onto another person's land. Also, a wrong done to another with force or violence.

Trial—A court examination of facts and law to legally settle a dispute.

Trial jury (petit jury)—A group of citizens who hear evidence and decide guilt in cases before the court.

Usury—Charging an illegally high rate of interest.

Vagrancy—Loafing, loitering, or being idle in a public place for a length of time with no regular employment and no visible means of support.

Vandalism—Crime of damaging or destroying someone else's property.

Verdict—The decision of a jury.

Violation—Breaking the law. Often used to describe minor offenses such as breaking traffic rules.

Void—Having no legal force.

Waiver—The act of giving up a legal right.

Ward—A juvenile who is legally protected by a guardian.

Warranty—A promise or guarantee of performance or quality.

Will—A legal document stating a person's wishes as to what shall be done with his property after he dies.

Witness—Any person who testifies before a court.

Writ—A written court document ordering a person to do or not do certain things.

Review Quiz Answers

Preview Quiz (p. x)

1. accessory	6. forgery	11. arraignment	16. negligence
2. larceny	7. jury	12. verdict	17. fraud
3. libel	8. assault	13. misdemeanor	18. embezzlement
4. subpoena	9. burglary	14. robbery	19. conspiracy
5. witness	10. slander	15. ordinance	20. arson

Review Quiz I (p. 12)

A. True or False

1. T	3. T	5. F	7. T	9. F	11. F	13. T	15. F
2. F	4. T	6. T	8. F	10. F	12. F	14. F	

B. Sentence Completions

16. criminal	21. subpoena
17. precedents	22. an appeal
18. felonies	23. judge
19. torts	24. common
20. answer	25. docket

Review Quiz II (p. 30)

A. Sentence Completions

1. Ignorance	6. Fifth
2. freedom	7. custody
3. rights	8. innocent
4. individual	9. trial
5. penal	10. jury

B. Defnitions

11. precedent	16. offender	21. habeas corpus
12. Bill of Rights	17. arrest	22. subpoena
13. juvenile	18. Miranda	23. evidence
14. hearing	19. bail	24. self-incrimination
15. juvenile codes	20. suspect	25. cross-examination

Review Quiz III (p. 56)

A. True or False

1. F	3. T	5. T	7. F	9. T
2. T	4. T	6. T	8. F	10. T

B. Matching

11. e	13. l	15. o	17. b	19. k	21. c	23. d	25. i
12. h	14. a	16. j	18. f	20. n	22. m	24. g	

Review Quiz IV (p. 88)

A. True or False

1. F	3. T	5. F	7. T	9. T	11. F	13. T	15. F
2. T	4. F	6. T	8. T	10. T	12. T	14. T	

B. Sentence Completions

16. open container	21. assault
17. assault	22. murder
18. suicide	23. felony murder
19. being a public nuisance	24. petty
20. federal	25. burglary

Final Quiz (p. 118)

1. a, c, d	5. b, c	9. a, c, e	13. a, b, c
2. b, c, d	6. a	10. a	14. b, c, e
3. a, d	7. b, c, d	11. a, d	15. a, b, d
4. c, e	8. c, d, e	12. a, b, d	

WALCH PUBLISHER

hare Your Bright Ideas with Us!

We want to hear from you! Your valuable comments and suggestions will help us meet your current and future classroom needs.

Your name_____Date_____

School name_____Phone_____

School address_____

Grade level taught_____Subject area(s) taught_____Average class size_____

Where did you purchase this publication?_____

Was your salesperson knowledgeable about this product?   Yes_____   No_____

What monies were used to purchase this product?

____School supplemental budget   ____Federal/state funding   ____Personal

Please "grade" this Walch publication according to the following criteria:

Quality of service you received when purchasing ....A   B   C   D   F
Ease of use..A   B   C   D   F
Quality of content..A   B   C   D   F
Page layout ....A   B   C   D   F
Organization of material...A   B   C   D   F
Suitability for grade level...A   B   C   D   F
Instructional value...A   B   C   D   F

COMMENTS:_____

_____

What specific supplemental materials would help you meet your current—or future—instructional needs?

_____

Have you used other Walch publications? If so, which ones?_____

May we use your comments in upcoming communications?   ____Yes   ____No

Please **FAX** this completed form to **207-772-3105**, or mail it to:

Product Development, J. Weston Walch, Publisher, P.O. Box 658, Portland, ME 04104-0658

We will send you a **FREE GIFT** as our way of thanking you for your feedback. **THANK YOU!**